Classroom Close-Ups: 5

Education For Sale

Classroom Close-Ups

A series edited by Gerald Haigh which tries to answer
the questions 'what really happens?' and 'what really
matters?' in education.

Classroom Close-Ups: 5

Series Editor: Gerald Haigh

EDUCATION FOR SALE

Eric Midwinter

Head of Public Affairs Units, National Consumer Council; Director of 'Priority', a centre for urban community education; and Chairman of the Advisory Centre for Education (ACE)

London   George Allen & Unwin Ltd
Ruskin House   Museum Street

ISBN 0 04 371049 2
      0 04 371050 6

Printed in Great Britain in 10 on 11 point Press Roman
at the Alden Press, Oxford

Preface

This book is an attempt to co-ordinate into a less irrational pattern the dozens of ideas buzzing around about selling education to the public in general and the parents in particular. In doing so, it tries to underpin the important points that educational salesmanship=parental education=home-school relations; and that home-school techniques are about improving children's educational attainment; otherwise it is nothing.

I have drawn on some seven years' experience in the 'parental' field, chiefly, but by no means entirely, in socially disadvantaged districts, and my object has been to build day-by-day practice into some sort of conceptual frame. Anxious that, in almost every case, proposals might be not recommended unless actually pioneered, I have sought illustrations from other parts of the country and from other individual practitioners. However, two groups have impinged so much on my professional consciousness and in so stimulating a manner that I feel it not invidious to mention them with genuine appreciation.

First, my own colleagues of 'Priority' and the Home-School Development Unit in Liverpool will not, I hope, feel ashamed thus to be nominated. Many, many workers and teachers in Liverpool (to say nothing of parents and children) contribute unknowingly to the following pages and to them my heartfelt thanks; but, at closer hand, I must in particular name four of my fellow workers on Merseyside: Jack Reynard, devastatingly sincere and loyal, eminently painstaking and open-minded, rocklike in his reliability and adherence to the work ethic; Eleanor Connor, sane beyond credibility, perceptive beyond proper acknowledgement and competent beyond excellence; Bill Thurston, balancing the sharpest of conceptual grasp with the shrewdest of practical know-how in cheerfully engaging combine; Sheila Cronin, bustling from achievement to achievement in merry and ebullient fashion.

The second group revolves around the charismatic leadership of John Rennie, the Community Education Adviser for Coventry. Without doubt John Rennie, along with his talented team, is now the key figure in home-school relations in the United Kingdom, and possibly in Western Europe. This brave assessment rests on that rarest of conjunctions: his thought-provoking and well-reasoned contribution to the theory of school and community linkage; and his inspirational and vitally inventive contribution to its practical implementation.

There are others — the Home-Link team in Liverpool's Netherley and Geoff and Lin Poulton in Southampton spring to mind — and all of us recognise that we grapple with a difficult and novel art-form. All those mentioned or alluded to would join me in inviting every teacher, in however small a way, to sample that art-form.

Two other points: I am grateful to Evans Brothers and Ron Dedman, Editor of the *Teachers' World*, for permission to reprint my two pieces of doggerel which I have used as prologue and epilogue. Both previously appeared in that admirable journal. Lastly, many proudly protest that their handwriting is puerile. As yet, I have seen none which, beside mine, does not look like the most delicately etched of copperplate. That shameful knowledge makes heartfelt my appreciation to Phil Rawcliffe, Secretary of 'Priority', for undertaking the preparation of the typescript.

ERIC MIDWINTER
August 1975

Contents

Prologue: A Cautionary Tale
(With sincere apologies to Hilaire Belloc)

The Tender Years of Timothy Shy
Were slightly incommoded by
His marked reluctance, on request,
To recognise with Vocal Zest
The simplest shapes and colours bright
Or pile his tumblers up aright.
In every field he Fell Behind
The others of his Age and Kind
All of whom could gaily prattle
Ere Timothy could grasp his rattle;
Nor did he greet with Deep Elation
His fellows in close conversation,
Refusing all their hopes of play.
His parents soon felt quite distrait.
He did not speak their titles daily
Nor, when they entered, gurgle gaily.
They sought help from a friend, whose foible
Was a special faith in Froebel
(Oft-times pronounced, of course, as Froebel)
And His belief in childish burble.
The kindly friend suggested they
Should contact soon their LEA
In order to present a case
And gain for Tim a Nursery Place,
For, so their informed friend contended,
Nursery Schools had been extended.
Thus, after Laboured Negotiation
Of a nature which defies narration,
Timothy Shy, it came to pass,
Joined a brand-new Nursery Class,
With vivid hues from wall to wall
And a Tropical Fish-tank in the hall.
Hopefully, his mother took him
To the school, but then forsook him,
Because, emblazoned on the gate,
She found a notice which did state
For every mother's steadfast guide,
'Parents Are Welcome to Wait Outside'.

Tim was therefore flatly landed
In spheres well-watered and well-sanded,
With climbing-frame and all the frills
Equipped to nurture Timothy's skills,
Under the eye and at the knee
Of a Nursery Nurse (NNEB)
Who offered him from Head to Toe,
An ample chance to learn and grow
And free himself into the bargain
And 'socialise' (excuse the jargon).
But Mrs Shy, a homely dearie,
Knew naught of modern Childhood Theory,
With access to the place denied
Wherein she might, at teacher's side,
Learn by what Method, to what Goal,
The Modern pre-school child's made whole.
So cudgelling her unsharpened wit,
His mother did the opposite
Of all the school contrived for Tim.
It was a Trifle Blurred for him.
Now school time very fast expires
Compared with hours before home fires,
And mother's influence, though perverse,
Was more pronounced than that of nurse:
Where they did 'number' she did 'sums';
'Free' art for teacher, the 'lines' were mum's;
They laid off letters: she went 'phonic',
Leaving Tim a confused and chronic
Case of academic schizophrenia,
In which his mother played the senior
And more crucial role, so that the cost
Was a Nursery Schooling largely lost.
Pre-schoolers should remark the thought:
'Hearth is Long: Cloisters Short.'
To give each child a Valid Start
Both Home and School must play their part.
And they must take a combined grip
To share in fruitful partnership.

PART ONE: WHY? IT PAYS EDUCATIONALLY TO ADVERTISE

Let one matter be perfectly clear at the outset. The question of home-school relations rests firmly and mainly on a professional appraisal of current educational knowledge.

Home-school relations have suffered from association with minor or even non-existent apologia for their existence. It is not some zany campaign of the ideological trendies determined to enforce 'participation' on unwilling mums and dads and create havoc for the poor old teacher as 'the tool of the establishment'. It is not sheer do-goodery, not least because, as *The Screwtape Letters* remind us, you can always tell who they're doing good to from the hunted look in their eyes. No, it is no updating of the Lady Bountiful role for teachers to distribute the lobscouse of educative largesse to the deserving, if reluctant, poor. It is definitely not social work, and nothing enrages the true home-schooler more than the suggestion that, by getting involved with parents, he is becoming a social worker or even, as I have heard it said, 'a nursemaid'. This is a dreadful foolishness. It suggests, even at best, that home-school relations are about 'problem families' or 'difficult children', whereas they are about all parents without distinction, albeit with considerable discrimination according to need. It is not just about good social relations either, and being on smiling, nodding and 'beckoning' terms with the mothers and fathers. This approach, coupled with the fund-raising, hand-lending at sports day element, is the pleasantest and most popular approach, but it is insufficient.

Of course, pieces of each of those items could be valuable. Parental participation – via the parent-manager – is a valid growth in popular democracy, and much to be encouraged. Similarly, home-school relations will embrace forms of educational aid to disadvantaged homes and, needless to say, pleasing social harmonies must be the prerequisite of any properly ordered relationship with parents. But prior to and beneath all that is the sheer *educational* reasoning behind the need to improve home-school relations.

It concerns the present state of our knowledge about the effect home and neighbourhood background has on pure educational attainment. The evidence is formidable. Let us take three representative neighbourhoods, the first with an average social composition, and the other two veering towards the extremes, as in Table 1.

Table 1

	Social Classes I, II, IIIa % of population	Social Classes IIIb, IV, V % of population
Normsville	30	70
Subnormsville	66	34
Supernormsville	16	84

Such figures are based on the Registrar-General's census returns denoting social class by occupation, with Classes I, II and IIIa embracing professional, managerial and clerical employees, and IIIb, IV and V encompassing skilled and unskilled manual workers. The figures dovetail adequately enough with other scales, for instance, the 'cultural' ones used by advertisers, and so on. Give or take 1 per cent, we can forecast the levels of educational attainment in such areas, as in Table 2.

Table 2

	Normsville	Subnormsville	Supernormsville
Poor reading ability at 7	30%	35%	20%
Selective or 'top stream' places at 11	25%	17%	45%
Number gaining five O levels	20%	9%	35%
Number staying in sixth form	19·5%	8%	30%
Number going on to higher education	7·5%	3%	16%

Now this does not glumly presuppose that, automatically, working-class children will do less well sholastically, nor does it necessarily avoid the genetic issue, whereby some would argue that heredity is a chief factor. A plethora of complex elements is involved here. A series of likelihoods exist in regard of contributory reasons. The mortality rate (national: 100) will be 90 in Supernormsville and 120 in Subnormsville; there will be 70 as opposed to 130 primary children per 1,000 population; the doctors in the one will have patients' lists of just over 2,000, and it will be near 3,000 in the other; there will be 2 per cent overcrowding and 3 per cent without standard amenities in the former, and it will be 18 per cent and 25 per cent respectively in the latter; average income will be 10 per cent above and 10 per cent below the country's norm; critically, average expenditure on education, libraries, and so on will be heavier in Supernormsville than the less fortunate Subnormsville, in the ratio probably of 10 to 7; and so forth . . .

Thus it is not the social composition *of itself* which explains the distinction. The explanation is knotted irrevocably into a web of social pattern making which both causes and is effected by that social composition. It will be remarked that pure and traditional educational measures — reading, O levels and what-not — were chosen to illustrate the point. This was to underpin the professional message. It is simply that we can no longer conceive of the school as an agency operating in a social vacuum. As teachers, we have had to come to the recognition that *everything* in the child's life, from the time of his birth, is affecting and subscribing to his education. The idea that the child is 'taught', solely and completely, in school must be abandoned under the weight of the fresh knowledge of the last ten or fifteen years.

In the past teachers have tended to see differences in terms of the mental and/or character differentials children brought into school with them. Admittedly, these cannot be forsworn, but we cannot escape acceptance of the fact that the sheer environmental context of each child is shaping and moulding him. This is, naturally, for better or for worse. Some home-neighbourhood moulds are, from the teacher viewpoint, 'good' and some are 'bad'. What is important is that, whether one approves of them or not, they cannot be gainsaid. The notion that some children are 'born with it' and that education is the task of realising 'natural' talent must be laid aside. Similarly, in the not so distant past, schools and teachers have, in recognising this fact, attempted to 'compensate' for the imbalance by improved staffing — ratios, resources, books and the like.

The sceptical point apart that this did not even procure equality of treatment, let alone offer extra assistance, this is an admirable directive. But it can never be sufficient. There are surely schools in disadvantaged environs which are operating as effectively as (granted our convention of the school) they are capable of doing, but the results are only tiny. The power of what is now being called 'the educative community' is so strong that, to phrase it in polarised caricature, where the home-neighbourhood pattern is 'wrong', the school, however brilliant its teaching, will get few encouraging results; and where the pattern is 'right', the school will prove successful, however disastrous the teaching!

With the neighbourhood — and especially the home — so important as a bonus or a penalty for each child, it behoves the teacher to examine that 'educative community' very closely. It is fairly obvious that where the totality of the pupil's experience is shaped and directed in unified form, then that is where the most successful results are to be expected. In a sense, this is what occurs in a stable suburban area, where the ethos, values, vocabulary and standards of home and school are likely to be in some fair degree of concert.

My own view has changed somewhat over ten years in this kind of field, operating principally in inner city areas but also in the executive belt. I was sentimental enough to believe that the kindly, heartening home, be it working class or middle class, was the key, but the hard school of day-to-day practice has taught otherwise. I am now, sadly, forced to confess that, on balance, the child in the happy, secure, interested working-class home is still at an acute disadvantage, academically speaking, even against the child in the dry, riven, sullen middle-class house. Simply, much of this is about know-how. Do the parents *understand* how the educational system works, so that their efforts, either unconscious or conscious, are supportive of the child?

Much of it is or can be unconscious. The 'elaborated coding' of the conversation, even if it's only marital rows, the *Daily Telegraph* bouncing in through the letterbox, the social intercourse with neighbours, friends and relatives, the books on the bookshelf, the air of expectancy and aspirations; these and many other socio-cultural items knit together to provide a supportive mechanism for the school, apart from anything which might be − as it usually is − done deliberately.

Consider this statement. In a large-scale survey of lower working-class parents, it emerged that 90 per cent agreed that it was easy to see the teacher or headteacher if they so wished; 80 per cent felt teachers were pleased to see them and were interested in their views; and 75 per cent thought their children were obtaining as good an education as children elsewhere.

This analysis reflected great credit on the schools and teachers involved, and it emphasises the point that parents are both concerned for their children's education and have a remarkably high measure of respect for the teacher. It was the other side of the medallion that was bothersome. Over 70 per cent of the parents, on questioning, were quite ignorant of the methods used at the schools and what exactly the teachers were attempting to accomplish. It might be added that only 50 per cent were public library members, and 30 per cent took no daily and 70 per cent no Sunday newspaper.

This combine of happiness with the school and unawareness of its detailed methodology is an odd state of affairs. In some ways it is very pleasing, but it also carries dreadful dangers. The parents are not passive or neutral. They have some effect; indeed, 46 per cent claimed, on this survey, that they helped their children in a formal sense to prepare for school. These were schools with terribly low achievement rates, despite all the effort and goodwill that prevailed. In brief, it was all that effort and goodwill which was *not* channelled and informed, so that the *entire* conspectus of the child's education was not at one.

It is difficult to imagine what dire consequences result from this possible scholatic schizophrenia, with the school doing its job and, either wittingly and blandly, or negatively and by default, the home doing another. Where parents have themselves been successfully through the process, they automatically, almost instinctively, are 'on song' with the school, providing the right background and props. Turning again to Supernormsville and Subnormsville, perhaps one of the key parallel statistics is the one which tells us that, out of every 1,000 adults in each area, only *40* in Subnormsville would have stayed at school beyond 16, whereas in Supernormsville the figure is a grand *130*.

All in all, the teacher must, at the very least and on the strictest professional grounds, consider whether he or she must examine that wider connotation of influence on the child in order to obtain for each child a 'full-fronted' and well-integrated education.

I must emphasise once more that this is not a job-remit for good works among the poor. Taking social composition alone, one must recognise that educational disadvantage is on a slope and not in a pool. There are not just 10 per cent disadvantaged, and it's hunky-dory for the rest. There may be that 10 per cent pool of extreme deprivation, but the slope rises to around the 70 per cent mark, with children relatively disadvantaged, until we move into that 30 per cent middle-class area where, so to speak, the children are overadvantaged. And that carries problems as well. I underline the point that home-school relations are for every parent. Whereas in Subnormsville the teacher may have to graft away attempting to improve the parent's ability to support the child, then, in Supernormsville, it may well be a question of lowering the temperature, of staunching the anxieties, of explaining carefully how home background affects education and of, in a sense, the minor role the school has to play. Having had a lot of experience of the one, and a little of the other, I am confident that neither task is the easier. As with children, so with parents, the teacher must be skilled in varying the principle according to need.

At least initially, one should, therefore, view the parent as being in a learner capacity, learning, with and alongside the child, how to obtain the best from educational opportunities. This knocks abruptly on the head the 'diluting the profession' scare, with its talk of auxiliaries and aides. There is little doubt that teachers have much to gain from parental help-mates, and provided the prior objective is recollected, no dilution will result; that is, if *informing* parents is the main aim, then the teacher retains professional status, and it may well be that, through a properly directed lending of assistance, the parent may learn swiftly.

Once the teacher sees that, in truth, the unit for his professional concern is the child plus the parent, and not the child *in vacuo*, then there is a chance that teacher-status may be heightened. If the teacher was viewed by society as the steward or convenor of the 'educative community', as opposed to the custodian of its younger members, then such a culmination might be brought to pass.

It is salutary to muse over the whys and wherefores of how parents came to have so passive a role. It really stems from the 'tutorial' or 'preventive' origins of public education in Victorian times. The children of the popular classes were, in bald fact, a social nuisance, just like paupers, the sick, lunatics and criminals. As with all those other categories of social casualties, there was a strong case for an institutional solution, with the school taking its place alongside the hospital, the workhouse, the asylum and the prison as a place in which a particular group of society's nuisances were housed, but housed in a positive attempt to 'improve' them. The then existing schools, the regimental barracks and, perhaps most important, the factory, all contributed to the theory and practice developed by Victorian educational administrators.

It was, therefore, a system operated in the belief that education was something that could be organised within the limits of the school without recourse to the outside world; and also in the belief that this was a good thing, too; that, on balance, it probably was sound thinking to remove the child from the malign or diffident influence of the home.

It has taken a long time for us to realise the shortcomings of the 'secluded' school and to recognise that 'education' is a thoroughgoing dimension of life, and not just those few hours a day for a few years sitting at the desk. The analogous field of health has concerned itself more briskly with this side of the matter; perhaps because the successes and failures of medical activity are rather more overt than those of schooling. From a similarly compulsory, institutionalised and autocratic approach in the nineteenth century, the public health and medical agencies have, under the pressure of circumstance, gradually and since the beginning of this century, tried to inform the public more and take them into their confidence. Quite simply, the institution could not bear the onus alone. Now mothers are able to handle with some verve and dexterity the health problems of their families, using knowledge and techniques which were, not long ago, professional mysteries.

Perhaps it is time for the teaching profession to raise its own status by taking a leaf from, as it were, the medical textbooks. A doctor or nurse is not necessary for many of the simple activities to do with health. These can be accomplished by the well-informed mother in the home. The dispensing of medicines, the dressing of minor wounds, the taking of temperatures, and so on — not only are mothers quite capable of undertaking such chores, but the professionals have too much pressure on their more sophisticated skills to be bothered and, moreover, they would regard such humdrum tasks as professionally out of court. Yet the teacher still often insists on trying to exclude the parent completely, viewing any attempts to help the child with reading or whatever as interference. The idea that, after the style of the doctor, one can delegate yet retain major oversight, has so far evaded most teachers. Thus they continue to busy themselves with the educational equivalent of doling out aspirins or sticking on the elastoplast.

Worse, by refusing to acknowledge the existence, good or bad, of 'education' in the home, the teacher runs the risk of opposed treatments, unlike the doctor or a public health worker who, by prescription and instruction, sustains overall control. There are many instances, then, of the educational equivalent of the sister spooning in one medicine in the out-patients' department and the mother trying a completely different box of pills in the home.

It is time we stopped looking at this problem in so gingerly a fashion. We really must take parents profoundly into our confidence. The occasion is ripe, for this is fast becoming the age of the consumer. The public (parent and child in concert, but not forgetting the rate- and tax-paying citizen at large) are the clients of the profession, and they deserve, in any event, the most fluent explanations possible. But this is but an added fillip to the urgent requirement of selling education to the public, especially the mothers and fathers, as a positive step toward inversed educational productivity and, by that token, improved value for the massive expenditure on education.

In essence, it is a monumental public relations task which faces all teachers. Somehow, and by every viable means, they must bind the parent into the whole negotiation of the educational process. One must not be facile about this. Eventually it will or should mean great changes in teacher-training programmes, in the allocation of personnel and resources, and so forth. It is a highly rational restatement of teacher-role when phrased in this ultimate manner. But it is not impossible, and there is now a welter of experience from all over the country about the day-by-day practice of home-school relations by ordinary teachers in ordinary classrooms.

The overall concept is, one must confess, a huge and visionary one, but the short-term and immediate practice is well rehearsed and to hand. Scarcely one suggestion made in the 'how' section of this book has not been tried, tried again and tried successfully.

Let the teaching profession, therefore, put education on sale.

PART TWO: HOW?

CHAPTER 1

'We don't want those dirty, bloody, smelly mothers in here with us'

Thus spake Ichabod. Or at least, an extremely attractive and competent, rather artistic young lady teacher in 1968, when the question of parents was raised in her staffroom. 'Our job', she opined, 'is to get the children away from their mothers and get some *standards* into them.' This lissom 23-year-old viewed the school rather as Beau Geste viewed his foreign legion fortress – as a haven of civilised valour and value midst barbarous hostility. But Beau Geste could, by and large, stay where he was or return to his metropolitan seat. Children are in school only five or six hours a day. They are in classes of thirty or thereabouts. The diffused influence of the teacher, especially when all the oddments of the teaching day are totted up, is relatively small. For the rest of the day, at weekends and in holidays, most critically for the years, often enough, before school begins, the child is under the influence of home, street and peer-group.

Certainly more teachers are more sympathetically aware of this than they were seven or eight years ago. The pupil, even on a schoolday, is *out* of school four times as long as he is in; and his sleep must be considered – two or three sharing a bed in cramped conditions as opposed to a snug ten-hour stint in one's own room adds another feature to the variance of the 'educative community'. More teachers are, therefore, growing concerned about those other nineteen hours of the day, to say nothing of the 165 school-less days.

Two or three years ago a young probationer, from a somewhat sheltered rural background and faced with a school in a notoriously vice-ridden and down-trodden district, said: 'I accept the principle, but how do I do it?' She was a light-year in front of the first teacher quoted, not only because she understood the problem, recognised its enormity and sensed her own inadequacy to cope, but also because she had lucidly differentiated between the argument about precept and the argument about practice.

So frequently, in discussions about whether 'dirty, bloody, smelly mothers' should be made welcome, the two are utterly confused, and the pursuit of the logic of the principle of home-school relations is mixed with queries about not having the time, not having had the training, being worried about discipline, and so forth. Important as these are, they only become important if and when the concept is accepted. So let the question be baldly put: do you, as a practising teacher, accept (or to what degree do you accept) the view that the child's continuing background, in particular his home background, exerts a lasting and constant influence on his development at school?

If the answer is 'yes' or 'yes, with conceptual reservations', then one can move on to tackle the 'but it's impossible/impractical' issues. And here we must, not too reluctantly, part company with the teacher who, Thomas Arnold *manqué*, still regards the school, alone and unaided, as the grand forcing-house of change. This 'holier-than-thou' attitude, this disdain for the power of extramural influences, must be borne in the spirit of that old doggerel on 'The Triumph of Rationalism'.

> When reason's rays shine over all,
> And put the saints to rout,
> Then Peter's holiness will pall,
> And Paul's will peter out.

And the first essential is to study the situation, as it were, historically. Obviously, either as class-teacher or headteacher, you must know the school, and its traditions, backwards. Few schools now have *no* home-school relations, however frail, and many have splendid links, especially at a social level. Naturally, one can examine these against the principle enunciated, and plan accordingly. Several avant-garde teachers have come to grief through attempting activities on the home-school front for which their colleagues, and indeed the whole ambiance of the school, were unprepared.

One has seen this in the curriculum field, and it is the same in the home-school field. It is no use crying over the spilt milk of a blinkered progressivism. It is anti-progressive, that is, counter-productive, to grasp for the moon and end up with the ideal in a sorrier state than hitherto. One may grumble lengthily and noisily about the reactionary character of staff or head, but the secret of realising an educational principle involves an acute tactical sense of how far advances may be made constructively and permanently.

The teacher must next understand the parents fairly thoroughly. This is a changing and growing knowledge for, of course, the way forward in this branch of understanding must itself follow increasing liaison with the home. There are two minor reasons and one major reason for this. One may find that parents are more conservative than teachers initially. After all, they have been bred for a hundred years in a heritage of handing children over to the professional teacher, and many are thankful that it operates so happily and painlessly. As the parent survey quoted in Part I demonstrates, parents were well content with the schools. It has sometimes been difficult (especially in deprived districts where practically every other service and amenity, from housing and transport to jobs and welfare, has deteriorated) to persuade parents that, although the school works overtly with efficiency and good temper, the positive partnership of the parents is a crucial ingredient. One must not be disappointed if, at first, the parent does not respond with cheery enthusiasm to the wonderful opportunity one thinks is being proffered.

Next, there may, admittedly, be the odd intransigent mother or father. When home-school relations are debated by staffs, it is often said that 'if the parents were allowed in, Mrs Bloggs might take over'. I suspect that there are less of these Mrs Bloggses, lurking at the school gate, surfeited with Montessori-like fantasies, waiting to pounce, than teacher folklore would warrant. Nevertheless you may be the unlucky one who would find the real Mrs Bloggs standing up.

Another piece of folklore relates to an ensemble of Bloggery. In the misty, distant past, there must, somewhere, at some for ever unnamed school, have been a parents' association composed entirely of pinko militants who, given a liberal inch, seized a Marxist yard, and attempted to turn the school into a Trotskyite cell. Now, in several schools, when the question of a parents' association is raised, up goes the aghast cry: 'It might be taken over by the Reds.' At the moment, according to some fearful commentators, the staffroom is likelier to be taken over by the Reds than the parents' association but, again, you may be the unfortunate one, with an unheralded Rosa Luxemburg watching and waiting on the nearby corporation estate.

In other words, one must try to sort out possible pitfalls among the parents before one embarks on a course of action, and this leads naturally to the major reason for 'casing' the parents. One generalisation has emerged from the work in the home-school field over the last ten years, and it stands firm and, unlike most generalisations, just about without reservation. The pitch and colour of the school-home attack must vary, imperceptibly and in detail, according to the cultural norms of the parent group with whom you are dealing. This follows logically from the idea of the 'educative community'. If the host community is to have free and fluid communion with the school, then the media for that communion must fall naturally and spontaneously and comfortably within the social and cultural purview of the parents.

What has been too easily labelled 'apathy' in the past has often been no more than the wrong brand of invitation failing. Teachers have blamed parents for being lethargic rather than themselves for being insensitive and insufficiently gifted in public relations. Secretaries usually transcribe into type one's fond scribbling with an obliging and cheerful lack of critical comment. Recently, however, I wrote something about 'How do schools expect father, after a hard day on the factory floor, having scoffed his meat and two veg. and put his slippers on, to scorn the delights of the telly and the evening paper, and sally forth to the school on a dark, rainy night in order to be told what a bum his son is?' For once, the typist reacted. 'That's exactly how I feel,' said she, 'we go to the school and they tell us what a bum our son is.' That, incidentally, was in a safe middle-class constituency.

Whatever else home-school relations have achieved during the last decade, one absolute truth has been revealed. Most (not all, but most) parents are vitally concerned about their children's education, and, *provided the school and the teachers are prepared to adapt the character of their home-school links to the character of the parents' subculture,* they will respond diligently.

This book, for its remainder, is wellnigh a paean of praise to that splendid truism. Having watched it happen over and over again in the most unpropitious circumstances, I am prepared to state that, given that kind of awareness, plus a little money, wit and energy, any school can obtain a 90 per cent response from its parents. I am not arguing, at the moment, that all else follows with tranquil ease, but merely that this degree of contact is possible on a regular basis.

It is not just a case of middle-class and working-class schools, with the cakes and tea of Normsville paralleled by the wine and cheese of Supernormsville and the hot-pot supper of Subnormsville. It is much more subtle than that and one must spot differences from school to school and from area to area. It has not always been possible for home-school officers to transfer ideas woodenly from region to region. At best, adaptations have usually been necessary.

I have had many happy connections with the vital home-school work currently leading the field in Coventry. Some years ago, I was deeply impressed by a lovely procession of several schools through the streets of their catchment areas to Primrose Hill Park, for a two-day Educational 'Happening' or Gala. It was most successful, and brought a legion of parents tumbling to join in and become involved. I planned a similar event for Liverpool, with some thirty-odd schools processioning from the Pierhead through the city to their various bases, again as a testimony to the work of the schools and their belonging to and in their community. But in Liverpool parades had a different connotation, all protests, strikes, rent disputes, and so on, with the Pierhead seen as a veritable Red Square of persistent rebelliousness. It

also carried a dangerous religious flavour. One teacher even went so far
as to suggest that, because the procession was planned for 14 June,
some might confuse it with 12 July, when the city's Orange Lodges
parade extensively in memory of the Battle of the Boyne. This was
none too rational, but it was a real enough response; we had misread
the mood, and we scrapped or rather reversed the idea, replacing it with
a motorcade which instead visited all the schools in turn.

Time and again, the requirement of a highly sophisticated monitoring
of techniques has made itself manifest. This is not to say that ideas
cannot be discussed or mechanics suggested. Rather is it that those
should continually be assessed against the life-style of the parent group.

Knowing the school and knowing the parents and their social context
are significant keys for success, but there is a third knowledge-gap to
fill. The physician must heal himself. Lenin said, 'Know your enemy',
and the enemy could be you. It follows from the emphasis on home-
school relations as an important professional attribute that the teacher
must always be the crucial agent. Thus it behoves the teacher to know
exactly how his or her sociological and psychological make-up fits into
the deal. Colleges tell us so much about the social background or the
intellectual development of the pupil. How well do we grasp that of
ourselves, the premier agents in the whole educative negotiation? As
much, if not more, than any other branch of the teaching craft, home-
school relations requires severe self-criticism.

Absurdly, some have suggested blanket solutions for home-school
problems, like all teachers living in the immediate vicinity of the school.
These total solutions miss not only the points previously made about
varying school and district cultures, they also omit recognition of the
varying personalities of the teachers. Some commentators propose that
all teachers should home-visit, and one hears of American districts
where this has been insisted upon. It could be more than unproductive.
The teacher must look inwardly and wisely at himself or herself. The
decision must be taken about what will happen when that teacher raps
that knocker. Will the face of the opener be wreathed in welcoming
smiles or will it crash in a thousand fragments on the doorstep?

The daily practice of liaison with the home must begin soundly with
and upon an amalgam of those three pieces of knowledge about school,
parent and self.

One must also, sadly, beware 'bad' practice, by which is meant
activities which are not even insufficient steps in the right direction but
clodhopping ones in the wrong one. It must be said that some schools
quite consciously deploy what overtly appear as promising home-school
plans to corral or contain parental hopes and aspirations.

There is the parent-teacher association, deliberately manipulated by
the head to avoid what he regards as possible confrontation. There is

the parent group which raises funds over which it has no jurisdiction or is recruited for labour-gangs about which it has no voice. A mute coolie with a full wallet would seem to be some heads' image of the perfect parent. I have even, incredibly, noted parents' rooms being furnished in schools, and then utilised as a kind of Bridewell for the mums and dads to prevent them from getting to grips with the school. As long as these exist, they can be interpreted as filling the bill. The parents' association which never goes over the fifteen or twenty membership mark because it is so boring and frustrating still remains a symbol that *something* is being done.

In real terms, it is the symbol of negation. The parents, the head might argue, could join if they wanted to, and that is no more than the truth. It is also no less than the truth, for those manoeuvres seriously delimit the proper expression of parental opinion and, more importantly, the parental receipt of information concerning the school.

Such 'repressive tolerance' is far worse than the well-intentioned, kindly home-school relations which, generally, one finds. These range from the affable sociability of everybody must come to the carol-service to the earnest desire of most schools periodically to inform parents — through reports, open evenings etc. — what their children have attained. These are pleasant and necessary respectively, but they do not begin to touch on the kernel of the problem. Why they are preferable is because the motives are more heartening and, by that token, they do provide a possible starting-point. From the carol-service might develop other sorts of invitations to hear, see and become familiar with the work of the school; while, from the bald logging of pupils' attainments, might develop discussions of how parents could become more positively engaged in the exercise.

My own opinion is that teachers should be in some form of contact with parents at least once a week, certainly in the primary school and as assuredly in the secondary school until perhaps (with the onset of puberty and the set pattern of examination courses) the coming of adolescence, when the whole question is altered by changes in the parent-child relationship itself. Even then, because of the advent of careers or college chances and indeed, because of the very posers raised by young adulthood, there should be only a mild slackening in the regularity of the contract.

This immediately raises the bogey of time. Now it would be easy enough to argue that, such would be the miraculous improvements in the pupils because of the beauty of the home-school relations, it would be time well and validly spent. That is not an unfair comment, but one must accept the present reality. Teachers cannot readily eschew their immediate responsibilities and cavort around as home-school liaison officers. Where possible, nevertheless, it should not be left to chance and home-school relations should be planned into the timetable. This would vary according to whether a school was primary or secondary or what aspect of home linkages was being pressed. It would likewise vary according to the skills and predilections of the staff. In some primary schools, a teacher with a particular interest in parental education has taken over a rich responsibility, rather like the teacher with a yen for music or games who teaches her subject through the school. Some schools now have an educational visitor attached or a home-school liaison worker appointed, whereas, at the secondary level, counsellors and teacher-social workers have been drafted. Elsewhere, a head and/or staff might feel that this professional responsibility should be shared.

There is no doubt that the scope for home-school activities is wider in schools where the staffing patterns are flexible; where, in secondary schools, there are interdisciplinary teaching groups, or, in primary schools, there is team-teaching and vertical grouping. Hopefully, one must look forward to the time when staffing ratios will be considered in the light of these professional duties, but, until that idyllic dawn, flexible but rational organisation will remain the answer. Also, in the longer term, that brand of activity where the parents more or less join the children in their daily round is the least upsetting. It is probably the most fruitful type of 'learning' for the parent; it could very much benefit the children; and the teacher is on location in the normal role of having oversight of the children.

The 'time' problem emerges when individual interviews, home-visiting, evening functions, the preparation of publications and the like become a heavy part of the teacher's job. This is where a sharing of the burdens, through shrewd timetabling and staffing interchange, along team-teaching lines, is necessary. In the past, many valiant pioneer teachers have merely added, with great generosity of spirit, such tasks to their existing ones. In the early days, nothing could be done about this, as such activities were experimental and *ad hoc*. Now that the case is made at worst to the point where every school arguably should have substantial if not all-embracing home-school relations, this can no longer be tolerated.

If this is to be regarded as a part of one's professional skills, like teaching maths or marking the register, then it must be formally recognised and as formally included in the job of teaching. It is lonely as well as laborious to go it alone with home-school relations. There is a limit to what the classroom teacher in isolation can achieve. It is much more a case of a head and staff joining together to the programme of campaign, just as they might discuss the reading scheme for the school.

Given an acceptance of the principle, given a knowledge of that intrepid trio of school, parent and self, given a joint enthusiasm or tolerance in the school and a certain availability of time and resources, what next? It has usually been suggested, from the experience of the last decade and a half, that one can draw up a gamut of home-school activity, ranging from the indirect to the direct. The indirect methodology has the parent, more or less, at arm's length (publications to the home, for example), while the direct methodology has the parent alive and well in the situation with a vengeance (parents working alongside children on appropriate projects, for instance).

According to the needs and anxieties of the parents, according to the current locus of the school on that indirect/direct spectrum and according to the teacher's own temperament and strengths, one should be able to select where to start or rather where to progress, or what assemblage of items might make for the finest home-school programme. It is intended to outline a variety of such activities, roaming from indirect to direct in that fashion, not in the belief that all teachers and schools should do the lot, but as a sort of market-stall of possibilities among which teachers might browse and choose.

CHAPTER 2

'*And I s'pose when we've finished this, the telly will come again*'

Let us begin with the school as a building in itself. We must reverse the process by which Victorian schools were deliberately built as gaunt forbidding premises, designed, like the Victorian workhouse, asylum, prison or general hospital, to incarcerate children and forbid easy exit to them and easy access to others. Even modern school building has, unconsciously, inherited some of that image. I suppose I have visited two or three hundred schools over the last twenty years, and many of them are hospitable and enjoyable places in which to sepend some time. So many of them, however, are inaccessible.

They are not, to begin with, always easy to find. They are badly sign-posted and sometimes hidden shyly away behind the church or lost in the heart of the housing estate. An alliance of patience and animal cunning will normally enable one to track them down, although, to digress slightly, I am constantly amazed why map-makers steadfastly refuse to denote the style of a school — it is so useful to know whether it's primary, secondary or what.

It is rather the actual business of entering the building, once found, which is the more daunting. School architects, more especially the Victorian breed, seem to have been assailed with nightmares of crazy Kafkaesque mazes. Tiny doorways vie with long, unfriendly corridors; blank, stony-faced walls compete with worn steps to nowhere. Some are like a cross between Troy and Jericho. Even when a doorway admits one, the eye is baffled by a Gothic idiocy of rooms, galleries, staircases and doors. One can poke around uneasily for quite some time, attempting to find bearings, although, when alone, one must usually resort to the sci-fi-honoured device of asking a passing child to 'take me to your Leader'.

I have lost count of the schools I have entered via the school kitchens or left via the school lavatories. Even in schools with which I have long experience, I occasionally walk confidently through that little door, and find myself in the playground again. It is not the teachers' fault that many of their premises resemble an agglomeration of architectural remnants borrowed from *Oliver Twist*, *Hard Times* and *Bleak House* and, of course, many parents, having attended the school, will know its layout well enough.

In simple truth, it offers no warmth of welcome. Many of the aged 'Parents must not cross this line', 'Parents must wait . . .', 'Parents can only see . . . by appointment' brand of notices are following the workhouse test into deserved oblivion; many schools have tried to be a little more sporting about their notices. But the whole fabric needs the treatment.

First, the outside of the school. The standard noticeboard sullenly announces the name of the school, perhaps adding the name of the head, and the name and address of the caretaker. Caretakers tend to resemble 'yonder peasant' — 'Sire, he lives a good league hence' — so that's not much help. Do something eye-catching with the noticeboard. If the clerk of works won't help, hand it over to your art department (or, if in a primary school and you've no sign-writers, the art department of your nearest secondary school). Draw attention to the name of the school. Invent a slogan and paint that up — not one of those antiquated corpy-Latin ones, but a ringing, authentic motto for this school in this area. Abjure the deadening blue and silver of the flat authority board; use your school colours and make for a distinctive board.

Time now to examine the mock-Catterick architecture of the building. It is probable you have a school badge. Provided it is not too rarified but is simple, gay, easily recognisable and in tune with the area, use it as your logo. Use it in every place and all the time. Make it as familiar to the parents as Oxo or the Shell shell. Have it on the noticeboard, on or over the entrance and as part of all notices inside the school. Having divided or having inherited school colours, stay with them firmly. Ensure that no one is in doubt about who or what you are.

If you have a long external wall, paint the school name in huge letters thereon. If you have a low-storeyed building, spell out the letters of the school title along the classroom windows. If you are in a tall, many-floored school, hang the letters vertically downward. Don't skulk behind the walls; emblazon the school and its name and its motif as much as possible.

Maybe you have a flagpole; maybe you could obtain one if you haven't. It might be on the roof or in the playground. Wherever it is, let the school flag flutter bravely from it. The school flag should be manufactured (perhaps the mothers would assist in this) in the appropriate colours and with the appropriate crest.

Turning internally, we have it on psychological authority that nothing is more off-putting than a blank door which one is supposed to open, but has no way of telling what is behind it. The most assured of people can be discomforted by that embarrassing challenge. This is why the glass-fronted foyer, if you're lucky enough to have one, is so encouraging: you can see what you are letting yourself in for when you barge through the door. Make your entrance as near to that ideal as you are able, even to the point, if weather permits, of leaving the door open. My own architectural taste would be for the entrance foyer having a very foreshortened drive to the gateway to the road, with playgrounds to the rear or at the side. This, once more, diminishes the mild trauma of fagging across a wind-swept expanse of tarmac wondering which door to employ and whether anyone is peeping at you.

Whatever else can be managed, the entrance area should be boldly and hugely sign-posted, so that no one should need to hesitate. It should also include informative notices about, for instance, the names and addresses of the school managers and governors. There should be an indicator-board, explaining carefully where various rooms or facilities are, and, needless to say, this is that much more important in the large, complex secondary schools of today. The school should work out a coding or routeway system, possibly having different colours for each floor or unit, tricked out with pointers and arrows, London underground style, so that visitors as well as children may the more smoothly move around.

Room and other doors should be more clearly marked than is the norm, and an attempt should be made to combine clarity and sureness of information with an overall and unified 'civic trust' appearance. As well as clear notices, each bearing the school logo, let us have cheerful ones and let us have child-designed ones. I have been amused to see schools where doorways have been enlivened by adding some inventive or picturesque illustration to the dispiriting bleakness of 'physics lab' or 'store room'.

A valuable analogy is the department store. It is hardly worthwhile a department store opening its (usually glass, see-through) doors unless its customers can be sent scooting swiftly hither and thither by a clear-cut series of directions. Oddly, the department store was 'invented' at much the same time, in the mid-nineteenth century, as the 'mass' school, but then the motivations were completely opposite. Today we are anxious to make the latter institution as tempting and welcoming as the former. Many schools, in particular perhaps primary schools, are nowadays a gorgeous riot of vivid colour and invention and, in many instances, it is no more than a matter of adding this existing creative resource to the needs of public relations.

A step on from this might be the site-improvement schemes extensively pursued on Merseyside and elsewhere. Organising children and eventually parents to perform such tasks has an educational rationale, and should normally grow from the curriculum. It should form a projection or reconstruction of a curriculum activity, and it should usually aim at giving children first-hand experience in civic aesthetics.

Wall-murals have perhaps been the commonest venture, for many schools boast, if that's not too optimistic a word, large bare walls. Occasionally these might be functional, like throwing targets or cricket wickets with pastoral backcloths, but even in these cases the work should be, if teacher-directed, child-oriented. Spectacular water-front scenes, splendid moon or space enterprises, exciting sporting pictures, zoological illustrations, pictorial circuses, histories of transport – these are instances of the genre. Internal walls are also, so to speak, tailor-made for this purpose.

Other schools, of course, have examined the possibility of site-reclamation, delving for small gardens or 'parkettes' out of pieces of near-derelict school land. Some have developed roof playground themes: one has had a nautical theme, with bunting, model steering wheels and yards of oceanic-looking ropes, and this became the location for a parent get-together, with the children providing a sea-going programme of songs, drama and artwork.

This has all proved most attractive to parents and to other members of the community. It gives the passing citizenry an insight into what the school is attempting and the school, in turn, demonstrates that it is anxious to make itself an asset loved and applauded by the community, and that it is eager to make its site as delightful as possible.

This admixture of educational artistry and social utility has much to commend it. I would foresee developments whereby balloons or captions might explain the rationale behind the material depicted. Further to that, the 'wall' newspaper-cum-mural, frequently changing, is a distinct possibility, with vigorous headlines telling parents what the school is doing in terms of concerts, visits, sports results or curriculum schemes.

The teacher-experts tell me it is preferable to 'size' the walls over before proceeding, and to work from scale drawings and either cut-out shapes or chalked outlines. A brisk supply of 'fire-salvage' and other 'seconds' in paints or the remnants of existing cans, plus the purloining of old shirts for little children to use as smocks, is the stock-in-trade required. One hazard of its success is the reluctance to change the wall mural or set garden-piece. This understandably grudging approach must be fought. Given a school with its notices, directions and other devices all bearing the same pleasing logo and house-style, it makes an exhilarating counterpoint to ring the changes on the rest of the decor.

It certainly makes for a lively fabric and draws an answering chord of response from the public; and it is all-encompassing of the age-ranges. It was a 6-year-old who said to me, as he solemnly painted his giraffe: 'And I s'pose when we've finished this, the telly will come again.'

Apart from the building, there are the teachers within the building. I have never felt compelled to join the endless numbers anxious endlessly to debate whether children should wear school uniform or not. I would, alternatively, like to be perhaps the first and only to discuss a uniform for the teachers.

The issue is authorisation, not authority. It is about 'recognisability'. Do you recall that advert where the burglar, in dairyman's rig, tells the housewife he's about to read the gas meter? It is something on those lines that concerns me.

It is not 'uniform' in the military or officious fashion that tempts me, but the fact that many who provide the public with a service – firemen, postmen, milkmen, and so on – are easily recognised. With more parents coming in, and more teachers moving out, it is a point worthy of consideration. My own experience of this has been with teachers providing advice points at holiday camps or in department stores. It is, in such cases, essential for the public to be able to identify the officers and receive some small guarantee that they have fallen into the right hands.

One has in mind the air-hostess rather than the lance-bombadier. The uniform must be eye-catching, debonnaire and attractive. Maybe the smock in a merry pastel shade would be an initial breakthrough, and by force of circumstance, this is beginning to materialise in the infants school. Obviously, the added bonus of the clothing being protective would help to push the idea. One's mind again turns to the store, the restaurant or the theatre, with a pleasing motif running through fittings, accoutrements and costume.

A smart smock or overall in the school colours and bearing the school badge would probably add to the image of a school keen to be seen, of a school eager to be, so to speak, dressed over all that it might serve its community more usefully and more pleasingly.

This idea could be – and has been – derived by those who consider it degrading, gimmicky and reducing teachers to the level of bunny-girls. That the onlookers would be so lucky! This criticism misses the point. The subject under review is the presentation of the school in as spanking and as life-enhancing and as vivacious a mode as the teachers, children and pupils deserve. It is true that, as district cultures and staff personalities vary, so will the character of this mode; it is equally true that professional people tend to confuse retaining a professional image with projecting an aura of pompous austerity.

CHAPTER 3

'A dazzling array of communication'

Rare is the school that sends no missive home. Whether it arrives or not may well depend on the vagaries of the pupil postal service, for, as a pedestrian around many schools, I have seen grid and gutter choked with such correspondence. Nevertheless, once the school itself is garbed and presented as happily as possible, school publishing is the next 'indirect' item due for appraisal.

One all-powerful and sorrowful fact must immediately be faced. The home is subjected constantly to a dazzling array of communication, created from extravagant resources by brilliant specialists. The colour television, with the allurements of its advertising; the daily blandishments of the *Sun* or the *Daily Mirror*; the persuasive technology of the supermarket or the mail order catalogue: these, and more, attack the senses of parents and children.

The cyclostyled sheet, poorly laid out and dull in content, is no match for the heavy artillery of the media. To be blunt, the grid or gutter might be an apposite resting-place. The teacher, the pupil and the parent are so important that the highest standards of design and presentation are deserved as well as necessary. Where possible, the reprographic services of the local authority should be utilised, but even where only the common-or-garden duplicator is available care and imagination can bring ripe rewards. I am sadly amazed by schools which, while properly demanding good standards from their pupils, are themselves slipshod and careless in publicity for the home. Where money is more freely on hand, obviously commercial aid may be sought, but, whatever else, we must get away from the funereal and, worst of all, unread image of many letters or notices from school.

If nothing else, an attractive letterhead, embracing the school logo and colours, can be designed and either purchased or home manufactured, and then used on *every* single item that goes to the home. It may well be worth considering uniform format and layout, provided this does not incommode the actual relaying of the information. On the same lines, there is much to be said for regularity. The sporadic and distantly spaced missive is likely to be left unread; by formula of layout and timing, the parent might come to expect, hopefully with some joy, the arrival of the school's communication. This presupposes some forward planning on the part of the school. So often letters or invitations are precipitated by a sudden urge to take the children on an outing or because some disciplinary issue has arisen. Parents must become habituated to the character and occasion of the school publication. The school should arrange its system of well-regulated communion and then insert information as it is appropriate.

It may be worthwhile considering the variety of publications open to the school.

(A) THE PROSPECTUS

The prospectus should be a full, illustrated and glossily produced account of the aims and work of the school. Aimed especially at new parents, it should offer them a very detailed picture of the brand of education their children will receive. Colleges and universities do this, and there seems no reason why schools should not follow suit. The pupil is every bit as important as the student.

(B) THE NEWSLETTER

This normally would be a simple publication with pieces on school activities and methods. It would be informative and, on the whole, teacher-centred, being used as a vehicle for straight-talking from teacher to parents. This might well be the medium, periodically spaced, for advising parents about the dates and so on of whatever activities are on offer. It then takes on the character of a regular bulletin. There may be special or supernumerary information or invitations to be forwarded to the homes, and they could well be added to this bulletin in the form of supplements.

(C) THE BOOKLET

This would be something like an occasional series. It might be to celebrate some event, such as a school birthday, jubilee or centenary, or a special school holiday or gala. It might report on a particular curriculum theme, such as reading methods or modern maths, or it might record the doings of some project or other. An actual instance of this has been a local environmental inquiry which led to the publication of a very down-to-earth and useful guidebook to a city district. Thus the community was able both to appreciate how the school was working and to obtain something tangible in consequence.

This category might include all the programmes for sports days, swimming galas, fetes, theatricals, dances, carol-services, concerts, and so forth. Once more, all should, at least in frame, be garbed in the school's artistic credentials and thus be easily recognisable.

(D) THE REPORT

I would include that much-feared and often-derided epistle among publications. It is usually the sole logging of the individual child's attainment to reach the home. From all that has been said, it will be realised that these reports should not be the severe, abrupt accounts of unhappy memory, ringing the changes on a well-worn list of platitudinous fault findings. The sonorous boom of an apocryphal one typifies the genre: 'The dawn of legibility in his handwriting only serves to demonstrate his utter inability to spell'; although that ponderous style is untypical – the curtness of 'only fair' and 'must try harder' may be more so.

I have in mind the full and chatty letter-report to the parent, which might be the basis for a verbal or, preferably, oral reply and discussion. Of course, like all these publications, it is more time-consuming, but the alternative is so unpleasant and futile that one might as well not bother. One might hope to see the teachers sharing a little more of the culpability. In a recent survey of hundreds of reports, only one item on one report read along the lines of 'I failed to interest your son in my subject'. One cannot expect such sackcloth-and-ashes penitence from all the profession, but a trifle more humility might ease teachers into valuable debate. Needless to say, these would all bear the authentic stamp of the school.

(E) THE CLASS JOURNAL OR PUPILS' WORK

Naturally enough, children's work is perhaps the finest way to interest and inform parents, for they find an immediate contact and identity with such material. A simple layout, essentially intimate and limited in nature, can make quite an impact, and it has the advantage often of intensifying the children's efforts. Sometimes individual endeavours may be sent home under, so to speak, non-plain cover. Schoolchildren frequently carry their bits and pieces home, but it is unexplained freight, by and large. If all had the same covering and each perhaps carried a brief exposition about the objective of the task, this could be very helpful.

(F) THE SCHOOL MAGAZINE

This is a popular and long-lived category of publication, and there are many splendid examples. It might be termly and, unlike the newsletter, it should tend to be child-centred. It should be colourful, gay and very readable, with an instant appeal that must make it a marvellous way of informing parents what is happening in the school. If it is the children's creative writing, the children's reports on school activities and the children's illustrations, then the whole might make for a very promising journal. I was recently astonished to see, in a competition for school magazines, that content, but not presentation, would be judged, for this seemed to me to fly in the face of all we now know about communications techniques.

A catalogue of possible items might be of assistance to would-be editors:

(i) *Children's work*: this should concentrate on everyday curriculum concerns, such as creative English, art, maths, science. environmental studies, recipes used in cookery, reviews of radio and television programmes received, and so on. Societies, clubs, out-of-school visits, hobbies and much other extramural action might also be reported by the children.

(ii) *Teachers' material*: this section might relate what actually is going on, and might even take the form of the term's prospectus. Staff changes, staff job-remits and responsibilities, information for new parents, a school calendar of forthcoming events, holidays etc., introduction of students on school practice to parents, all manner of administrative and practical information – all this and more should be considered.

(iii) *'Outsiders'' contributions*: it is extremely helpful when others connected with the school are encouraged to contribute. The lollipopman, the caretaker and groundsman, the school dinner staff, the cleaners; these are directly concerned with the school, but there are also others whose articles I have read in school magazines, such as the unit policeman or juvenile liaison officer and the milkman. Then there are 'official' folk to invite, like the school managers and governors, the school nurse and the local HMI or authority advisers.

A collation such as this could prove a valued support in attempts to keep parents informed. And there is another vital ingredient: the parents themselves. More and more magazines are including parental contributions, while some are being handed over, kit and caboodle, to the parents to edit. Other members of the community – old-age pensioners, shopkeepers, social workers, and so forth — might be recruited as features writers.

A further list of pointers might be of some aid. First, one must be very careful about style. This refers initially to vocabulary. That awful language of 'schoolese' ('the school First XI again enjoyed a mixed season . . .') must be avoided and editorial staffs (except where children's work is concerned) should be ready to adopt the argot of the subculture they are serving. The classical rotundities of the traditional school magazine could well be lost in districts which are used to a vigorous proletarian patois. Vocabulary must, of course, be chosen cautiously, and the golden mean between intelligibility and condescension is not easy to find. The same directive on style also applies to layout and design. A mock-up is essential to ensure the magazine fits together in unified manner. So many teachers insist on collecting the material, then trying to knock it into shape. The shape must be insisted upon first, with decisions taken about what goes where and how long it should be. Bold headlines and well-placed illustrations all help.

A guide to presentation in many areas must be the popular press. Some school magazines and newsletters have been constructed in the form of the daily newspaper, to add a fetching air of familiarity. Good-sized print and, if possible, large pages can be of assistance. One should not deny additional items like school calendars and/or supplements or crosswords, competitions and lucky numbers, with prizes to fortunate winners. All this requires the most attentive emphasis on pre-planning.

A second pointer relates to follow-up. Of all home-school liaison, indirect endeavours like publications are the most difficult to evaluate. Questionnaires, perhaps appended to the magazine, have been found useful. Amazingly, one such venture in a downtown area evoked a 100 per cent response the following day! Mock Gallup polls at the school gate or at appropriate school functions might serve that same purpose. These enable the editors to judge which sections of the journal are succeeding and which not, while they also give a proper air of importance to the proceedings. Parents feel quite pleased to be asked.

A third directive is an underpinning of the ground point that the business must be conducted with clockwork precision. Deadlines must strictly be kept; pieces must be courteously commissioned; delivery and distribution must be regular and punctual. One empirical piece of evidence is that publications of this kind are, in fact, delivered, and they don't get dumped. Because the products are worthwhile and overtly of high quality, a little more care is taken of them, while they also gain from being something the children feel is very much part of them.

The same sense of 'possessing' which, in my experience, has meant little or no vandalism of, or graffiti on, wall-murals and other site improvements, holds good. Children don't vandalise or abandon the things which they like or of which they are proud. The magazine, like the wall-mural, must 'belong', and then it will be cherished and protected. I know of one mother who, on holiday, always contrives to leave her school magazine on train or plane, in order for a fellow-traveller to share the pleasure, such is her secret pride in the school and its publication. Few journals inspire that kind of devotion; all can endeavour so to please.

Beyond all this, the over-riding objective must be sustained. All publications must aim at providing lucid and readable material by which the parents will improve their grasp on the school process, that, in turn, they may encourage the children more intelligibly.

CHAPTER 4

'We're on our home ground'

A next possible step, and one requiring much more of an element of carrying the campaign directly to the community, is the public exposition of the school at natural focal points. A natural focal point is simply a place where people gather informally or, more precisely, non-formally. It is a well-rehearsed sociological truth that individuals pursue a fairly heavily worn path through their day-to-day affairs which brings them intermittently into group contacts of one kind and another.

That is a more-or-less ornate way of saying that folk get together spontaneously and without prior invitation. It is often argued that these natural congregations are more valid and less artificial measures of social discourse and popular opinion than the bureaucratic channels. It is wellnigh possible to 'map' the non-formal pattern of a district, taking into account among others the betting shop, the bingo hall and the boozer as spots where viewpoints are made, tested, transferred and altered. It is a commonplace piece of advice for parents — or indeed education officers — seeking information about local schools to do so in the launderette rather than the education department office.

A school must be very alert to the possibilities of this network and, of course, this would be a feature of an earlier point about teachers knowing their catchment area thoroughly. At the very least, if schools are to be assessed in the launderette, one may as well ensure that the adjudication is not based on faulty testimony.

That is, I repeat, the very least. Of much more fundamental impact is the chance to inform and educate at the social hubs of the neighbourhood. It is an opportunity to tune in on the locality's own wavelength, rather than to rely on somewhat synthetic approaches within the institutionalised climate of the school. As with any wavelength, perfect tuning requires a sensitive touch and an empathetic ear. It must be accomplished in sympathetic and watchful fashion and, amidst the variety of ideas offered in these passages, nowhere is it truer that one must always adjust carefully to the value system of the host culture being served.

At base, this is another series of devices for raising the level of awareness among the populace of education in general and your school or class in particular. The commonest, but not exclusive, instrument is some type of exhibition. The school sets out to explain its viewpoint, its aims, its methodology and its results by parading its wares on the community market. Many schools are happy to exhibit schoolwork in the school and to invite parents to come along and pay their respects. This technique is the reverse. Of course, it does not deny the place of the school as an exhibition centre, but it argues the case for the school sallying forth to press its product on parent and ratepayer.

It is probably a less expensive method than the professional publication, and it has, so far, proved not only highly effective but capable of wide variation. Here is a list of the social locations where, in my experience, this technique has been successfully employed:

(i)   The supermarket, the shopping precinct, the department store or row of shops.

(ii) The factory canteen or shopfloor, the works (or other) social club.

(iii) The church hall, the library, the doctor's waiting-room, the health clinic, transport termini or even the buses themselves – utilising those little oblong advertising slots.

(iv) Leisure amenities, such as the bingo hall, the park, the holiday camp, the pub, the cafe or snack bar.

The school must go where people are. The above list is by no means full – football grounds and cinemas are but two more places which could and should be used but, to my personal knowledge, have not been. But that list does begin to spell out where mothers and fathers spend their out-of-home-time, that is, shopping, working, at leisure, and so on.

One point is that they are more relaxed. Much of the experimental work has been evaluated by interview techniques, and most general responses reflect this air of relaxation. I was concerned with a twelve-day exhibition in a city department store which attracted 10,000 visitors, a record for that emporium. Some 500 interviews were conducted, and the message was clear. At last, people said, we are finding out what the schools are really doing, and – the phrase crops up over and over again – 'we're on our home ground'.

There is not the same sense of occasion, with perhaps attendant anxieties, as with paying a visit to the school. It is interesting that, out of that sample of 500 just quoted, half were in the store and realised that an exhibition was in progress, whereas the other half had come specially for the exhibition, but were content to do a little shopping as well.

This bisection is quite symbolic. It reflects the joint nature and character of the enterprise. Few persons are all that single-minded about their shopping or their business; they are often quite happy to allow other conversation, light and serious, to intervene. They are not being asked to gaze at education as the sacred ark of the covenant, placed far away and on high. They are being invited to accept education as part and parcel of their everyday lives. They should be pleased, but not amazed, to find the local school in the works canteen or the coffee-bar. Being on their social circuit for a purpose, they are happy to be distracted and diverted, temporarily and briefly, by another purpose, provided it is something as vital to them as their local school, and provided the diversion is provided with energy and flair.

As well as different loci for such operations, there are varying modes of presentation. The exhibition has been already mentioned, by way of illustration, and it is a straightforward enough means of exposition. It can stand, on shop wall or in bingo hall foyer, as a constant reminder of the presence of the school. It does not need to be manned, and it has proved very popular with viewers.

One or two points need to be emphasised. As with the internal fabric of the school, the school colours, logo or other identification must be used uniformly, and the same size and format of exhibition frame or poster is advisable. One must be careful to shun the temptation of exhibiting just 'good' work or just artwork. It is the average traffic of the school which needs to be translated to the public, and that covers the breadth of the curriculum. Explanatory captions are usually necessary and one should be as likely to find, say, a cartoon strip interpreting modern maths as the finest still-lifes the art department can muster.

Change is of the essence. Where a similar site is in perpetual use — such as a row of shops — a weekly or fortnightly exchange is desirable, in order to avoid any note of mustiness or tattiness entering into the venture. Shopkeepers and others have been remarkably co-operative in such enterprises. It can, of course, provide an added attraction, and help keep shops and so on brisk and busy. I can record two instances in separate districts of groups of shopkeepers complaining bitterly because they had not been included or invited to join in the scheme. A valuable projection of the static portrayal of the school's work is the 'live' demonstration. Teachers frequently claim that the process is more important than the product, yet, on open days, it is devastatingly the product which gets the airing. This can in some way be compensated for by taking children to appropriate vantage points to demonstrate school activities and methodology. As with the exhibition, it must be explained. In the most successful cases, the teachers have cleverly interposed spoken interpretations as they conducted their lessons, and/or provided a simple handout, lesson-note or programme so that the onlookers could follow progress more intelligently.

Again, it is your average class and your average lesson on activity which is necessary to offer a realistic picture of the school's daily round. The colour and excitement must come from the style of the presentation, although, hopefully, the school's daily round would be replete with colour and excitement.

Thus I have seen 300 shoppers assembled in a department store to admire an infants' physical education lesson; I have seen a crowd gather on the concourse of a teeming shopping precinct to witness a class presenting cookery, pottery and dressmaking; I have seen a host of some thousands on a recreation ground closely attentive to a display of dance and musical movement; I have seen workers in a factory canteen enjoying improvised drama along with their roast and two veg.

It is even more exhilarating when the parents may join in the activity. It is a fair generalisation that, when parents can be, concretely and practically, induced into and through the actualities of the process, then they may learn more swiftly and deeply. So if these 'live' demonstrations can offer that opportunity, one gains compound interest. Examples that spring to memory are a group of ladies, all armed with shopping bags, intensely engaged in a series of modern maths calculations and, on another occasion, Saturday afternoon promenaders around a huge tree in a suburban park busily trying their hands at 'child' art.

What immediately became apparent was the variable drawing-power of differing activities. As might have been predicted, those curriculum or extramural enterprises which parents are traditionally invited to view — music, dramatic work, dance — attracted consistently larger 'gates', whilst those with a conventionally harsher image — maths, geography, history — were sparsely attended.

What lessons were to be learned from this? In the first place, if parental relations are to be taken seriously, then one might reconsider the amount of creative arts on the timetable. The olde worlde speech day reflects the dilemma. Music and dance-drama may have to struggle for existence through the year, but, come the arrival of the VIPs, it is the school choir and orchestra or the school dramatic society who mount the stage to represent the school. Rarely is a pupil asked to step on to the rostrum and calculate a quadratic equation or discuss the rate of rainfall in Bolivia. Perhaps the very appeal of the creative subjects should dictate a higher spot for them in the curriculum hit-parade, particularly if they become interwoven with other subjects in cross-disciplinary style.

That is a point for syllabus construction rather than home-school relations, but a second lesson followed on from this. Much of the curriculum effort with which I had been associated had been in the urban studies or social environmental field, and this sometimes had the austere character personified by the earnest pupil, clipboard in hand, solemnly counting the manhole-covers or television aerials in some mean street. We discovered that when the creative arts were added to the pupils' first-hand grasp of urban local issues and were deployed by them to express that grasp, then both the social awareness and the aesthetic expression of the children mutually climbed to its highest degrees of quality.

Having had the pleasure of operating closely with a theatre-in-education team, it is of that specialism that I can write most intimately. It soon occurred to us that theatre techniques could, as well as boosting mundane classroom action, probably propagate the gospel of such activities as well. The most successful illustrations I have enjoyed have been with infants. Three or four covers on 'reading with mum' and 'maths with mum' have drawn very respectable crowds of mothers to watch their offspring participate in amusing theatre episodes which, covertly, demonstrated to the mothers the methods used by the school to teach reading or mathematics. With a back-up pep-talk by headteacher or adviser, plus a display of books or other materials, this can be pleasurable and informative. Another instance, with rather grander objectives, have been a couple of socio-drama gaming situations for parents and other adults, contriving to place the participants in experimental situations in regard of educational issues. These, too, can be effective, although my own preference is for those which involve the children *per se*.

Teachers will argue that this is a sophisticated technique, and that is true enough. Nevertheless, if tackled simply, it could become a part of the stock-in-trade of home-school relations. If teachers could portray reading, maths and so in story-form or symbol-form through characters played by children, it could help parents to visualise the problems and processes involved. I have touched mainly on theatre techniques, but the modern dance version of how religious education is taught or the musical playlet based on how languages are taught or an exposition of arts and craft showing how science is taught are not beyond visualisation. Such instances approximate nearly enough to modern interdisciplinary practice to be tenable. No one turns a hair at a jazz version of Jonah and the Whale or Joseph and his Coat of Many Colours. What is needed is the message, the musical of other 'caption', telling 'why' — why the subject is being pursued and why certain methods have been selected.

Another angle of the question of 'live' demos is that of the procession. In several city areas now we have been able to judge the colossal impact of a school procession on its catchment district. It unashamedly borrows traditional clerical practice and, despite its proletarian traits, I suspect the children's procession would not go its happy way amiss in the most salubrious and refined quarters.

One makes no bones that it scarcely delineates in detail the work of the school. Granted, it could, on parade, demonstrate once more the artistic beat of the school, with music, dressmaking, theatre and crafts to the fore, and with the possibility of physical education or modern movement being exhibited with mobile gusto. An enterprising secondary school might, for instance, allocate a float to each of its departments and, for the delectation of a wondering public, demonstrate the mechanics, the hardware and software, of each discipline.

But the procession has a broader and yet a deeper meaning than that. It is a testimony of educational witness. Again, like the religious 'walks' or campaigning marches, it is a forceful gesture of solid educational presence. Literally, the school procession beats the bounds of its catchment community. The school takes to the streets and passes the houses of the children and their parents. It is saying, in its processing, 'We are your school; we belong to the community, and movingly and proudly, we present ourselves to you.'

Music helps. A school band is a brave sight, and a public address system, for music and for oral exhortation, is a grand asset. A school song, especially if it has local reference and if its lyric and melody has the 'feel' of the region or locale, is a splendid addition. In Liverpool we persuaded The Scaffold to write for us a catchy theme-song with the devastatingly simplistic title 'Schools, Schools, Schools, Schools'.

> Schools, schools, schools, schools,
> Schools, schools, schools, schools.
> School's not just for little kids, school's for everyone.
> Especially for mums and dads, schooldays can be fun.
> Unity, community, they are the golden rules;
> You'll make us all much happier if you support our schools.
> School's the place our children spend the best part of each day.
> And we're inviting everyone to watch us work and play.
> Come along and give a hand, that is the golden rule.
> You'll make our town a better place, if you support our school.
> Be it ever so humble, there's no place like school.
> For the bits of rough and tumble, there's no place like school.
> Schools, schools, schools, schools,
> Schools, schools, schools, schools.

With a school brass band or a strong youth choir to back it, it proved as 'efficacious' as The Scaffold's own notorious 'Lily the Pink'. The school banner or other heraldic device should be borne aloft and, a humdrum point, it pays to tell the police. Once or twice a term should do the trick nicely, with the school, as ever, 'recognisable' through its own colours, logo and motto. If regular processions are planned, an overall theme might be chosen to add some unification to the parade. It might be a curriculum principle, perhaps representing stories read or geographical locations studied. I recently enjoyed a centenary celebration in the midlands where teachers and children carried off a Victorian-style procession with compelling *élan*.

The urban artisan area is well used to processions, and both children walking and citizens spectating take kindly to the idea. Some teachers, in the interests of educational evangelicalism, may have to take a deep breath and shelve their embarrassment. The extrovert teacher, and they are not unknown, is a willing enthusiast. The procession, quite simply, draws more massive crowds than any other home-school exploit and, in a phrase, no one has so far clocked up a failure.

Next there is an amalgam of the procession and the 'live' demonstration with the formula of the 'mobile exhibition', probably more suitable for the secondary than the primary school. This consists of attempts to transport samples of the school's methodology to varying locations. It avoids the possible shortcoming of the static longer-running performance that only those who, say, use that supermarket or this railway station will reap the reward, while, in forcing home, so to speak, the lesson of lessons, it is more sharply pointed than the procession itself.

It can take, thus far, two forms, although other forms may evolve. The first is when, to quote an actual instance, a coachload of pupils do the rounds of a factory canteen, old people's clubs, bingo hall, and so on with a fast moving twenty to forty minutes 'gig' on their school's work. It is presented theatrically and as a dramatic unity, with music and other art-forms as possible vehicles. One school promoted its own opening and closing chorus for such a venture. As with the more formal 'live' demonstrations, a handout, perhaps in the style of a theatre programme, is helpful.

The other form leans on the other mobile excursions into education, notably in the early childhood field. The Playmobile or Playbus, a travelling unit for pre-school children, and mobile toy and children's book libraries are already in existence, but an inventive secondary school might pick up cheap an old public service vehicle, such as a bus or an ambulance, or a good-sized second-hand caravan. After the fashion of the gas board or the army recruiting drive, it could be moved from pitch to pitch, depending on where people were most heavily congregated.

It could proffer general information about the school; it could be temporarily taken over by each department or school activity; it could exhibit some interdisciplinary theme, with, for instance, a summer jaunt being tricked out with sun-wear and school-made ice-cream by courtesy of the home economics department. Its suitability for older pupils has another advantage, in that secondary schools often cater for a wide geographical area with consequent difficulties in reaching all their client-population. A line of shops may serve the complete catchment of a primary school, but secondary school 'zoning' is both wider and more variable. The mobile unit can be at the nearby gala, outside the local football ground, in attendance at one of the 'feeder' primary schools, or simply on a street-corner. These types of mobile 'living' exposition we have dubbed the 'cavalcade' approach.

Exhibition, 'live' demonstration, procession, cavalcade: they tot up to what, for many schools, would be a mammoth leap in public relations and, yet again, the question of time might be raised. The answer lies in rational organisation, in establishing a long-term plan and allocating duties and responsibilities accordingly. One teacher might be given overall charge, or those interested might be put on a month-about roster. For a smallish primary school one might reckon that a weekly change of material at one set of exhibition vantage points (local shops or the local pub), a termly procession and, say, a major annual campaign of one week's duration would sufficiently test the stamina and creativity of the staff. With the wider resources and wider needs of the secondary school, more sustained pressure may be both possible and necessary. With sound organisation, an on-going regular 'cavalcade', in addition to the allotment proposal for the primary school, might be suitable.

Many of these ventures call upon teachers to perform esoteric and weird functions, remote from the daily grind of chalk on board and tick in exercise book. The negative point might be pressed, tongue only lightly touching cheek, that these are all 'out-going' activities. One could justly say to the teachers who fear the mass ensemble of parents *within* the school that these adventures into educational show-business are for them. Similarly, to those who moan of never seeing the parents they really want to see, here is an opportunity to seek them out in their own milieu.

Alternatively, all these expressions of the school's wherewithal would gain fruitfully from the actual participation of parents and, especially in processions and, as described above, in 'live' demonstrations, this is already occurring.

CHAPTER 5

Home-School Harry et alia

A further chapter must be added to deal with a natural outcrop of the exhibition-demonstration style of educational salesmanship. This is the need for straightforward advisory points. Many of the foregoing descriptions have concerned the heightening of the general level of educational awareness, but there are naturally many individual posers which require individual resolution. This is often an authority and should even be a national matter, but the school may frequently be able to assist, for educational problems are resolutely individualistic, chiefly relating to the one child, unique in his or her educative context. Indeed, during most prolonged education advice experiments, success has been such that joy has been muted. Advisors have felt overwhelmed by the numbers and depths of the questions and have realised, sombrely, that very many families have such problems that they either do not know how to find redress or, knowing of the whereabouts of the education office, they are loath to become entangled with its bureaucratic coils.

Thus an advisory point might be added by the school to several of the exhibition modes previously suggested. Literature needs to be available in some profusion and with maximum clarity, and a school should endeavour to build up a small library of reference material. A mail-an-answer service can be a useful device, with the promise of a researched answer later. Parents – the parent-manager or governor or committee members of the PTA or local branch of a parent organisation – may help man these advisory points, and the local education office might be pleased to contribute materials and even an officer for this purpose.

An 'ask me' counter when the school is on show at the local works or department store or in the local park or as part of the 'cavalcade' caravan could be helpful, but one must emphasise the objective 'prolonged' when speaking of the success of such a service. Too often an 'education shop' has been established in some obscure cranny – a small, uninviting tome-lined niche at the back of a grandiose library was one – for a few days, and, when the response has been tiny, opponents have excitedly shouted of 'failure'. One must realise, with this as with

all other home-school links, that parents must be given manifold time
and opportunity to acclimatise themselves to new aids. One must work
hard to create that degree of familiarity.

The holiday camp has been particularly successful as a location for
the 'education shop', despite forebodings that people would resent the
incursion of solemnities like the latest reading scheme or Dienes
Apparatus into the idyll of a holiday. Over a number of years, advisory
teams have been pulled inside out by a persistent battery of
questioning. The holiday camp may be a trifle outside the compass of
the ordinary school, but one interesting lesson is worth recalling. The
holiday is probably the only time the whole family is at leisure
together, so that interviews, sometimes lasting as long as two hours,
with mother, father and child, have not been uncommon. The 'leisure'
syndrome may be copied by the school, which might search out
locations in the community – the new rash of leisure centres or the
annual crop of fetes or, where appropriate, holiday resorts and haunts
– for this type of exercise.

This involves another issue relevant to advisory points but also to all
the other out-going activities, and this relates to the appropriateness of
locations to specific approaches. Even with exhibitions in shops,
refinements are necessary. The social whirl of the fish-and-chip shop
calls for the large, quick message, while the slower plod of the clinic
or the doctor's waiting-room allows for more detail. To begin with,
fish projects in the fishmonger's and meat projects in the butcher's are
obvious instances, plus, for example, sports news in the local. Take the
department store. The exuberant window-display or the 'demo' of the
latest culinary weapon mean that similar occurrences culled from
education – the project in the window; the teacher and pupils and their
cookery lesson – can be offered without contrivance. It all gells fluidly
with the nature of the beast.

In the holiday camp it was found essential to adapt some of the
Butlinesque razzamatazz, with lots of coloured, gas-filled balloons, jolly
opening ceremonies and cheerful competitions. The factory canteen is a
natural arena for the showbiz or cavalcade approach, carrying with it
some traits of 'workers' playtime', while the bingo hall or allied agency
permits most effectively of the brisk, buoyant ten-minute pep-talk at
the interval. In districts where staple industries like mining or car-works
or shipbuilding cater for the majority of the fathers occupationally it
could be a great scoop to make contact with that one workplace and
encompass most of the parents with a sole technique.

In other words, chameleon-like, the school and its representatives
must fade into the terrain where they find themselves. Actually, it is
not quite camouflage, for the school must be immediately recognised.
Here again, the question of the school 'house style' – its colours and

other heraldry — must be remembered, for all these endeavours should be suitably presented. Here again, the recognisability of teachers — the debonnaire 'uniform' issue — is important, particularly as and when teachers find themselves taking to the streets. To discover — as one recently was able — a pre-school advisory point in Coventry's branch of Mothercare is a token of the need for education to become absorbed into the community. Not hidden, but assimilated; it must not disappear, but it must not stand out uncomfortably like the sore thumb of a grey-suited, grey-faced educational expert among the swarming nattily attired thousands in the holiday camp or behind the department store counter alongside all the winsome, charmingly accoutred shop assistants.

The Hillfields district of Coventry has annually had an 'Educational Happening' for its dozen or so schools, and this has proved a good, all-round illustration of the genre. It is a weekend (Friday/Saturday) event, with celebrities like Eartha Kitt or Joe Mercer to perform the opening honours. It has a long, winding procession to the local park where, around a large central arena for a broad series of displays and other 'live' activities, there are ranged marquees with school equipment and materials on display. 'Happening' tee-shirts and other goodies are for sale. The schools are *en fête*, and massive multi-racial crowds stroll happily and watch with patent satisfaction.

So much more of this is possible. Some schools have adapted the conventional school concert as a medium for telling what the school is and does. Imagine, in place of the traditional music festival in the town's assembly hall, a staging of *The Rise and Decline of the Beatles* with, as well as the musical thread, an analysis of the lyrics and some acute dramatisation, some social historical display and comment, some survey, with illustrations, of changes in fashion, and the assistance of various other curriculum ploys. Imagine, alternatively, the town's main street at Christmas with, instead of the crass predictability of commerce and local authority laying on their flat and tedious yuletide trivia, the schools, the teachers and the pupils, creating their fresh Christmas image of music and drama. Imagine the derelict site, either the overgrown patch in country suburb or the demolition scar of the conurbation, reclaimed, beautified and perhaps made functional by a team of pupils.

Whatever the enterprise, a main consideration must be pre-publicity and follow-up. Whether it is a procession or an 'education shop', the local folk need to know that it is happening and, for many events, it is useful if customers or spectators have a little something to take away with them, by way of a handout or leaflet — it might be an information sheet on a point raised by a questioner at an advisory point or a brief explanatory note on a curriculum demonstration. This transports us back to the field of publications, for the same ground-rules apply. Well-designed, smart advertising in the familiar school-home style is important. One cannot expect much from the scrappy, hastily painted poster for the school fete or play stuck on a meat-hook in the butcher's shop. The publicity must be carefully planned and as delicately timed: the early warning shot some time before to alert the potential client; perhaps — depending on the importance of the occasion and the degree of togetherness of school and home — an interim booster; and then the final reminder just beforehand.

For most school events there is little to beat the word-of-mouth. If a good parent team exists, they might be recruited to ensure that that word does spread from mouth to ear, inviting them to take responsibility for a group of parents. The children are a safe bet, as long as they are convinced of the rightness and the value of the event. If they are excited by it, they are likely to excite their parents. I recall one child who persuaded her father to close his restaurant for the morning to attend a school function. And once the programme of action is smoothly and regularly programmed, it can become second nature for parents to attend or support. That is the summit of home-school ambition: for the parents to need little or no cajoling, but, like fire-horses at the sound of the bell, to respond instinctively to the haunting call of the school.

Another aspect of publicity must be the local press and the local radio. Happy is the school with a personal contact in such potent places; persevering must be the school which hasn't. The ultimate is a small weekly column in the local paper or spot on the local radio station, but it takes skill to obtain and then sustain that luxury. Nevertheless, the press and radio are not averse to carrying school news, especially when it has verve and a pungent flavour. Apart from actually imparting information, press and radio have two subsidiary functions. One is to prove, over and over, that schools are newsworthy and are or should be an exciting part of cultural existence; the other is as a morale-booster for all concerned, the sheer joy and mild vanity for the teachers, parents and children of seeing themselves in print or hearing themselves on the air.

A final tip on the publicity side is to personify the theme. In Liverpool, some years ago, we produced Home-School Harry, played by a leading theatre-in-education exponent. An impudent, personable character, in a distinctive green and orange suit, he became the spearhead of the home-school assault. For example, when we organised a 'Support Our Schools' week for some thirty-six city schools, he led the motorcade (referred to on page 22 in another connection) and, in street and playground, starred in a short playlet depicting the home-school link, with the aid of his fellow-actors. Incidentally, this was, over one school day, repeated thirty times in a tight schedule of military precision.

At each school Harry left a joke-certificate of his attendance and, from each school, received a gift, often a model or collage representing him, or a personal present such as a motorcar or a nine-foot dinosaur. That was in 1972 and during that week, ever since and emphatically when similar 'intensification' weeks are organised, Home-School Harry has been in substantial demand. Mothers, not only children, hail him in the street, not infrequently when he is out of his full regalia. Infants grow anxious in case he has died. He has opened all manner of occasions and attended all manner of functions. During the week in question, the thirty-six schools (comprising some seven or eight thousand children) laid on almost two hundred functions among them, and there was a total attendance of nearly eight thousand adults during those five hectic days.

Home-School Harry is in the laudable tradition of Sunny Jim, Mr Cube and World-Cup Willy and, as a symbol, he succeeded beyond our wildest fantasies. Every school should have one. And one or two schools have moved in that direction by creating their own mascot, related to the school or its area. The next step would be to breathe life into it, and persuade teacher, child or parent to be cast in the role. It might be a group *aux* Wombles, consisting of delegates from each of the three educational branches. Either way, a mascot could become the school's coat-of-arms, its badge, its flag, its letterhead, and so on. We had Home-School Harry on our brochures and all the children had a Home-School Harry sticker.

The story of 'Support Our Schools' weeks, together with the tale of Coventry's 'Educational Happening', made another salutary point. In both these cases, under the aegis of authority-sponsored officers, groups of schools were co-ordinated for fuller impact. Without some external initiative, it is not easy to organise thirty or forty schools in such a fashion, but it is worth three or four schools, with existing close contacts, considering a federal approach. A self-evident example might be the comprehensive school, in a fairly tight catchment community, such as a redevelopment estate, joining together with its six or seven primary 'feeders'.

Banded together, a group of schools can pool resources for firmer impact in terms of publicity and all-round impression. A not inconsiderable point is that everything is less expensive if purchased in bulk or, more liberally, one might afford together what alone could prove prohibitive. I have found myself dealing with orders for 15,000 brochures, or 20,000 stickers, or 10,000 sticks of rock with 'Support Schools' printed through them (not 'Support Our Schools' — you can only get fourteen letters through a stick of rock), or 20,000 triangular pencils with 'parents', 'teachers' and 'children' printed on each side of the triangle. The red triangle has, in fact, come to act as the overall symbol of home-school relations. Coined by A. H. Halsey, director of the Educational Priority Area projects, 1968—71, the 'Teaching Triangle' denotes the two-way learning-teaching process of parent, teacher and pupil: we have had, for instance, thousands of red triangle stickers manufactured. Quite simply, one school can rarely manage that kind of relatively extravagant refinement, but it could benefit from a joint endeavour. Incidentally, this also applies to publications; in both Liverpool and Coventry there have been interesting experiments with printed 'covers' of general publication into which schools or classes could insert their own independent material.

The issues raised in this chapter have been advisory counters, relating locations appropriately to techniques, publicity, 'personification' and co-ordinated efforts. Although the mainstream of the illustrations used have referred to 'out-going' activities, almost all these issues can also be associated with the following chapter, which examines 'in-coming' activities, whereby the parent is tempted to enter the school. It would be otiose to repeat these suggestions about advisory points or publicity or mascots when the parent in the school is considered. Suffice it to emphasise that each of those directives hold good inside as well as outside the school.

CHAPTER 6

'It'll end up with the children waiting for us to come out of school!'

Dazed with the kaleidoscopic motley of our colourful campaigning through the high streets and byways of our district, the parents should now be softened up and ready to cross the school portals; which is an indirect reminder that not every school, let alone every teacher, would be expected to try every technique, and the same applies to the plethora of proposals for welcoming the parents into the school.

It is time, too, to recollect the object of these exercises, namely, to give the parents the fairest balance of social assurance and educational information for them to support their children's efforts in school. And that might mean persuading the university-educated professional man of the benefits of learning through play, as well as explaining to the harassed working mother the benefits for her son if he were to stay on at school.

Having the mothers and fathers on the premises has certain apparent advantages, but there are two initial drawbacks or, at least, possible problems. On the one hand, the school is the school is the school. It is not as amenable to radical cultural alteration to suit varying cultural contexts; it is simpler to move out of the school and, through exhibitions or processions of differing typology, modify the approach to the subculture concerned. The school, like it or not, is more constant and uniform in character across the country. On the other hand, in many intramural contacts the confrontation is a face-to-face one. Some teachers may feel embarrassed on parade down the main roads, but at least they need not be drawn into converse with individual parents. On the school premises another kind of acute discomfort might present itself when teacher and parent meet in what might be termed an eyeball sandwich. There is hardly any escape from that one-to-one collision.

That is to put it sourly, but, if we are concerned with raising the level of educational sensitivity in each parent, the challenge of direct and in-depth teaching relationships must be faced. It is here that the teacher's role adopts an 'adult education' feature. The teacher, at these times, becomes adult tutor. The teacher is teaching the parent to understand the education system, so that the parent can, with and on behalf of his or her children, make independent and clearsighted choices and offer well-informed encouragement.

This is why the 'indirect-direct' routeway of home-school relationships is a very meaningful description. The 'indirect' approaches and techniques are essential. They create the atmosphere in which solid school-home liaison becomes possible, but, except for some advisory work, most of the activities so far outlined have been 'indirect' in the sense of not treating with the individual parent intently.

It will have escaped no one that many of the proposals for outdoor educational salesmanship were merely taking what often happens in the school into the streets. Obviously, there is still a ready place for all the concerts and exhibitions *within* the school that its staff and pupils can muster. Once, however, a school gets the hang of projecting itself at all these natural foci in society, the mundane carol-service or summer fair may become rather small beer. Those teachers who argue that, because the parents are invited to the sports day or the nativity play, home-school relations exist, are deceiving themselves or, at best, operating on loose, even alternative, definitions of home-school relations. This does not mean that the spring jumble sale or the prize-giving or the dramatic society's annual classical excursion should be abandoned: it does mean that the objectives of these exercises should be cautiously and clearly catalogued, and not confused with the ideal of the well-informed and supportive parent.

That much said, it might now be helpful to consider three formulae for a closer correspondence of teacher and parent intramurally.

(A) THE PARENT CHIEFLY AS SPECTATOR

Given that it is, for one reason or another, appropriate to utilise the school for concerts and exhibitions to which parents are invited as spectators, how can these be sharpened in terms of direct parental benefit? I think there are four major answers:

(i) *The curriculum message*: a point, previously made, must be underlined. It is important when producing concerts and the like to sweep broadly across the syllabus. Ensure that all facets of schoolwork are illustrated and, what is more, ensure that this is made plain to the audience, by captions, address or handout. The curriculum 'message' is too frequently left (if even envisaged) to herald itself, and is thereby lost. The parent may admire the gorgeous costume in the school play or the enthralling scenic effects, without realising not only that pupils were engaged in the preparation but how it fitted into the developmental process of that particular subject or activity. The curriculum light is hidden by all those bushels of exhibition for exhibition's sake.

An infants school of my acquaintance has used 'festivals' for this purpose. Its 'festival' roster is a full one, running from Hallowe'en and Guy Fawkes at intervals over the school year. Each festival becomes, in reality, a centre of interest or project with almost all aspects of schoolwork introduced. Come the appointed day, the parents arrive to see, hear and taste (it is a school where much infant cookery is in vogue) the products, with careful, and not distractive, explanation of methodological issues. The concert-cum-exhibition in miniature thus becomes a working model for the parents' delectation and inquiry on a colourful, regular and ever-changing rota.

There are a hundred other ways of writing the school's approaches into the exhibition or concert format. Even the conventional play can be made much more the 'project' for several departments of the secondary school, not in any subsidiary or downgraded sense, but with each aspect properly discussed, organised and then projected.

(ii) *The local slant*: it is absolutely crucial to give any such activities a local or subcultural slant. I have recently been impressed by the number of schools in urban areas who have laid on old-time music halls for the local populace, and this has brought them tumbling into the school-hall in their hundreds. For bringing parents and other citizens into the school, it has few equals, and it can be most diverting. With food and drink to match, it can become famous entertainment, but it may be more than that. Again, some infant and junior schools use a curriculum theme — London, the sea, a colour — as the base for a song-chainer, tricking out the medley with a variety of methodological items.

Another by-product of the old-time music hall is its self-evident attraction for old-age pensioners. Many schools, primary and secondary, thoughtfully promote concern for old age on part of the school's wherewithal. Old-age pensioners are very much part of the educative community of a school; they are a splendid repository of curriculum content for the children; and a wonderful source of help to children, as well as a proper object for their generous concern. The grandparent is but one stage removed from the parent in the perspective of home-school relations; many may have the time to enjoy, or be thrown by force of conditions, into a closer relation with the child than the mother or father. It is worth teachers recalling that parents are the hub but not the entirety of the child's social wheel.

Multiracial districts have offered a series of delicious
illustrations of the school being *en fête* and, although the sight of a
class of West Indian children solemnly singing 'The British
Grenadiers' for visitors is not yet unknown, the distinctive nature
of varying ethnic cultures has been picked up smartly by many
teachers. It would be galling if they did not accept the same
diversification from the indigenous population. The brass band or
the Morris dancers in the schools of mining and allied areas is a
pleasing instance, but, as yet, the school play still exists too often
as the breathless gabbling of some arbitrarily declared classic,
received with polite clapping from lines of uncomprehending
uncles and aunts.

Schools are now developing differing musical styles, with
'groups' and other excursions into the modern idiom, just as they
are experimenting with 'pop' art 'junk' sculpture and modernistic
craft and pioneering several exciting theatre-in-education ventures.
One of my own favourites still remains the solid artisan area where
the school has a forty-strong ukelele band. Its appeal is catchy,
unworried and constant.

(iii) *The mecca of gaiety*: these attractions should, as well as being
informative in themselves, act as the diversionary sprat to catch the
educative mackerel. Frankly, they may be utilised as decoy ducks,
and the same applies to a panoply of activities ranging from the
now extremely popular disco for parents (and pupils) to the
winey-cheesey parties that go so excellently in many districts.

These are pleasing enough in their own right, either for social
reasons and/or to raise a pound or two for the school fund. It is
just that, simply, no opportunity should be lost. As long as it is
not too abrasive or blatantly disruptive, the chance should be
taken to sell education. Techniques must vary. The ten-minute
fireside chat, previously mentioned as having worked well enough
in the interval of a bingo session, is not likely to win through at a
disco, where a tape-slide sequence, perhaps with a 'carousel'
projector, may be more in keeping.

Having made the point in several sections of this book that the
school can be an off-putting institution and that the school should
move out into the vaster arena of the community at large, it is at
this juncture that the converse of this must be urged. In short, as
well as outflanking the school's inhibiting traits by 'out-going'
activities, teachers should also endeavour to de-institutionalise the
school. The advice on noticeboards and such was of that order,
and all the social panorama of bingo and disco, of jumble
sale and spring fair, of folk evening and rose queen, of carol
concerts and swimming gala, all of this should, if correctly handled,
have some cumulative effect.

The prerequisite – it must be said again – of sound home-school relations is parental confidence, and nothing is likelier to inspire that assurance than what probably has the austere image of their own childhood being replaced by a mecca of gaiety, comfort and non-embarrassment.

(iv) *The parent joining in*: the fourth issue is the corollary to be added to most of these home-school precepts. The sooner the parents are participants, even organisers, the better. This happens at sports days and athletics meetings and with costumes for plays and building extra amenities like swimming pools: once more, one does not cavil at this, but one must distinguish between assistance and involvement. If a group of perhaps specialist tradesmen among parents undertakes a task like putting bookshelves in a room designated as a library, that is fine, but it tells the children little about woodwork and the parents little about the school.

When the objective is informing parents then involvement is critical. I have very much enjoyed school cabarets or variety where a troupe of parents have shown their paces, either as a chorus-line *en bloc* or by taking parts in pantomimes or other performances. In these instances the mothers have become part of the same disciplinary and educational regulo to which the children are subject. At several exhibitions, I have inspected the art or craft productions of parents and, again, they have moved through the process with their children. Some teachers have commented interestingly on the manner in which mothers, coming late and pristine to art, follow the same developmental pattern as young children. The same obviously applies to musical and other curriculum elements, and the more parents can 'mix it' with the pupils, the more effectively will they learn.

(B) THE PARENT CHIEFLY AS 'ATTENDER'

This last rider, about parents performing or otherwise joining in events for which normally they are spectators, leads naturally into a section on other calls on parents' attendance, perhaps with some involvement. These should commonly evolve from the standard occasions of school protocol, the open day or evening and the speech day. Now of all examples of home-school links, such events as these are most likely to chill the heart of the parent and evoke amusing reminiscences in any staffroom. A personal favourite of, sadly, seventies vintage is the invitation to the parents attending their annual open evening, almost as if in celebration of that hit-song from *The Pyjama Game* entitled 'This is my once a year day'. The invitation opened unpromisingly with 'when queuing to talk to your child's class teacher', and then continued 'it would be helpful if you could arrange yourselves in alphabetical order'. What could be more insensitive than to invite parents coldly once per annum into a strange institution, then impose upon them so bizarre a charade?

Prize-givings and speech days have even been the subject for television plays and have been comically featured in films. The celebrity guest is often selected *because* he is quite apart, vocationally or culturally, from the school or its community, so that the Earl of Here or the Vice-Chancellor of the University of There will go through their inane, because unrelated, set-piece on the adventure of life as the serious plot, with their own failure to win prizes at school as the comic relief subplot.

It is pleasant to enrol successful or famous persons to help a school. It is good for the ego; it is good for publicity; if they are the right choices, it is good in itself. Previous mention was made of Eartha Kitt and Joe Mercer in Coventry. In Liverpool, when Home-School Harry was operating in 'Support Our Schools' week, he threw a huge party for the parent-teacher-pupil delegations of several schools, some five hundred people in total. It was a little like a party convention, with each school having its name-banner flying over its table and with each school tucking into a cake with its name picked out in pink icing. The honoured guest was Ken Dodd and he made that a most memorable occasion for everyone with his own style of spectacular comedy. The fact that he understood and was able to articulate about education as it affects the ordinary mum or dad rather more shrewdly than the Earl of Here and the Vice-Chancellor of There was a pleasant bonus.

The theme should again be clear. It was a party, not a prize-giving, and Ken Dodd inexorably grew from and now contributes substantially to the culture of the party-goers. In many urban areas the tradition of the street-party is still very strong, and should be utilised. One remembers how, come coronation, royal wedding, world cup or cathedral opening, streets and tenements are decorated, with religious, political and even sporting differences temporarily forgotten in the joy of dressing the road overall. Out come the mountains of sandwiches and jellies, by the hundredweight. A couple of years ago I was privileged to be present at a party secretly planned and given to the head in his own school to celebrate his birthday, with parents, staff and children enjoying a superb high tea.

This 'cakes and ale' style must be developed in many more schools, and replace the dreary *longueurs* of the speech day. Districts with a different social caste, where sandwiches and bunting might be considered a trifle *outré*, could evolve their own type of jamboree for such occasions.

The same applies to the open day or open evening. Some of these are still managed along all but theological lines, with a bell ringing at intervals to indicate the end of interviews and the visiting parent feeling something of the confessional in his brief exchange with the teacher. These need to be very much livelier, with the parent made to feel comfortable in the situation. The parent plays too passive a role, especially as in a case which occurred with a colleague recently, when the teacher flipped over two sheets by mistake and offered a report on the wrong boy.

The school has so many facilities which could, properly used, make it a place which people wanted to visit. One of the advantages of the 'community school' is that because people are there for all kinds of leisure or social reasons it is easier to establish another, educational, liaison with them. There was an earlier discussion of 'natural focal points' in the community; much needs to be done to make the school just as much a 'natural focal point' as the launderette or the bus station. With such acceptable facilities, it should be not all that difficult to accomplish, provided the school's heart is in the right place.

For instance, will the school, if it finds the authority in a willing mood, run a licensed bar, either regularly or on an occasional basis? Will it, once more granted a gracious authority, use its kitchens and dining facilities to provide meals or light refreshments for parents and other citizens? Food and drink is no extravagance in home-school relations. It very fluently lubricates the fundamental social interplay. During a seven-year period helping organise home-school relations, I reckon a major outlay was solely on cups and saucers. Revolutions are built on cups and saucers. Cups and saucers permit tea and coffee to be dispensed to visiting parents; the cup cheers; tongues are loosened, tensions are relaxed.

Two years ago Fulham were fortunate enough to meet nearby West Ham United in the FA cup final. The streets of Fulham were spanking and gay in anticipation — vainly as it transpired — of the team lifting that coveted trophy. I was told of a teacher in a Fulham school who had no idea why the streets were decorated and asked wonderingly in the staffroom why it was so. This brand of insensitivity to the subculture on the part of a teacher is most unsatisfactory; one might go so far as to label it unprofessional.

It is, then, against that social and cultural frame of reference that the following thoughts are deliberated upon. They list a number of modes for engaging the individual parent educationally and within the school.

(C) THE PARENT CHIEFLY AS PARTICIPANT

An interesting phenomenon has been noted during recent intensified efforts to attract parents into schools. Like most natural phenomena it looks, in retrospect, as if it should have been easily predicted; it is the tendency for parents to respond to a 'class' invitation more hearteningly than a 'school' one. This has now been witnessed sufficient times for it to become a useful guideline. In several instances I have known of schools organising a pleasing enough programme of parental activities – low-budget cookery, dressmaking etc. – with fairly disappointing results. On experimenting with each class or form or vertical grouping inviting its mothers separately to a 'class' event, the response has improved dramatically. It has frequently done so in absolute numbers: I may quote a case of a school with ten classes attracting only fifteen or eighteen parents for what seemed a pleasant series of school-based events. Turning to the separate class attack, they rarely fell below twenty for each group and, not infrequently, every family was represented.

The sense of identification of the parents with their children and with *their* teacher is obviously very strong. Several schools now ensure that all children appear in the school entertainment, but, in a sizeable school, even this contribution may look a little lost to the parent. To join your child and his/her teacher and his/her friends in their classroom is a more intimate and telling experience. So true is this that it may serve as one of several reasons why secondary schools have, on the whole, been less successful than primary schools in the home-school field. The conventional reason given is that the children, as they approach adolescence, naturally begin to grow away from their parents a little. This is a partial explanation. Another reason must be that, with the change to a more subject-oriented timetable and with (ironically, the more so the more 'progressive' the school) so many options that timetables become individualistic, group identity is not as keen. Some pupils may not be taught at all by their group tutor or form master, let alone spend the day entirely with one mentor.

It is interesting that, where secondary schools (usually for other if equally valid reasons) have moved to the first one, two or three years spent in team-taught, mixed ability, randomly selected and interdisciplinary groups, parental liaison is a little easier to foster. It may be that the large area served by the big secondary school and perhaps the sheer size of the school itself may be off-putting. Suffice it to mention that secondary schools, anxious to develop sounder home-links, should put their own house in order and attempt to preserve that close sense of identification.

The 'class' session has normally taken one of two forms. The more popular has been the entire class inviting all its parents in for an afternoon or morning session, and asking them to watch eagerly and, where appropriate, join in the lesson or topic, attempting to see the problem, the task, or the skill to be exercised from the pupils' angle.

Refreshments are available, and sometimes the work is given that special twist to accommodate the learner-parent. From some of the original endeavour in this approach, the generic term 'coffee morning' now tends to be used for this venture, although tea in the afternoon is equally admissible.

The alternative is to invite a small group – say, two or three sets of parents – to join the class for a day, seeing the class function from dawn to dusk, having lunch in the school, and so forth. This may be especially valuable where, on the physical side, space is very confined, or where, on the social side, the teacher is anxious to develop or inaugurate rather close relationships with the parents. Space is sometimes used a little too glibly by teachers as an excuse for avoiding parental contacts. In practice, there are few classrooms which cannot be made accessible to a group of parents for a couple of hours with the minimum of fuss and classroom management.

The parent, in these situations, begins to see in detail the problems set her child and to face them herself. She is able, in some cases for the first time, to appreciate not only the way the child develops educationally, but the enormous quantity of expertise which the teacher must handle. This is an exercise in eye-opening. The parent's eyes are widened, but the teacher learns something about the parent, and about the parent in relation to the child; indeed, I have known teachers claim to be the chief beneficiaries of the 'coffee morning'. The children gain in seeing home and school harmoniously in partnership, and usually find some joy in this.

Once more, it must be noted that primary school children will sometimes go to extreme lengths to persuade parents to come along. Secondary pupils may sometimes be extreme in their reticence about parents visiting the school. This may partly be blamed on the onset of puberty, but there could be an internal reason to do with how comfortable the pupils feel with the school, especially as a context for their parents. I well remember occasional embarrassments when my parents visited the school; I never suffered so acutely when accompanying my father to a football ground, cricket match or theatre. It could, in part, be the institution.

Once under way, it is important to sustain regularity of this kind of visitation. To begin with, it might be sufficient for all parties to place all classes on a weekly roster, that is, one class per week. Initially, there will be snags and help will be required from other teachers. The question of the invitation must be considered; it has normally been the case that a nicely printed outline with the child adding his own wording has been satisfactory. The question of tea and biscuits or other refreshments must also be resolved.

Gradually, a once-a-week rota might be constructed. This has certainly worked rewardingly in one or two Coventry schools as well as elsewhere. One or two classes choose a special day of the week so that, over the week, all the classes are served. The Wednesday becomes Community Day for class four. It is the day when parents, relations and other friendly neighbours and visitors are asked along. It is a 'guest' morning-afternoon. It is an educative-cum-social enterprise, at which parents can see how things are organised and become acquainted at near hand with the process.

Regularity is the key. So many parental ventures are sporadic and haphazard. Parents must become accustomed to the 'feel' of being in the school, and an irregular attachment is of no comfort. Apart from this it enables planning to be much smoother, and it leads inexorably to the next point.

If the get-together is regular, be it weekly, fortnightly, half-termly or even termly, teachers can programme accordingly, so that the induction of parents is spread over the breadth of the curriculum field. For example, on a weekly basis the parent could quite simply pursue alongside the children some curriculum theme, whether it be a geographical probe, a piece of language or creative work, a new phase in the maths scheme of work, and so forth. The 'festival' approach described earlier was, in effect, an exercise of this kind. Many parental visitations on the school are hit and miss; they get a rather static snapshot of what is happening that particular time or, as likely, what has been contrived to happen at that time. The parent needs to sense the unfolding nature of the educational flow, and may well be able to do this only by periodic dips.

All this may lead on to what I once termed the 'Everest of home-school relations', namely, the child-parent project. This requires more of the parent than that he or she is an onlooker, who occasionally lends a hand and does bits and pieces with the pupils. It is much more full-blooded. It designates parents and pupils together as the normative teaching group, which then attacks some curriculum centre of interest together. Interestingly, we have seen some success with this as an evening function when every, say, Tuesday evening, for four, five or six weeks, a class has returned to school with its parents to continue a piece of work. Evening attendance stood healthy comparison with daytime registrations, apart from attracting a larger number of parents than children. Daytime or evening, if some arrangement can be made for little ones from these families to be cared for, this can help numbers. This, of course, applied to several of the activities in the home-school field. Incidentally, evening ventures of this kind are invaluable for fathers and working mothers who are not free during normal school hours.

It is at this juncture, with the parent moving through the actual process alongside the child, that the likelihood of proper understanding is highest. There have been combined groups of this kind researching into local issues or presenting an interplay of drama, creative writing and music making on a localised theme. The assurance of the parents can be increased when they note that their experience is relevant to curriculum content. It boosts their confidence if they can make a substantial contribution to work on local history, local folklore or local social mores. They may find that there are several common social denominators — television, advertising, seasonal events — which are parent-centred as well as child-centred.

The teacher provides the professional direction and the battery of skills required. The parents operate in a concretised way and, as well as gleaming something of how child development burgeons, they may feel gratified and comforted by the knowledge that they have contributed of themselves.

It has several times been said that when a teacher is uncertain whether to label an activity as 'home-school relations' or 'curriculum developments', it is a time for rejoicing over a victory. It indicates that the mood has changed from helping the parents because they are influential in the 'educative community' to recognising that influence positively and developing from that point. Instead of just telling parents how the system works, the parents have become accepted subscribers to the system.

There are many possible versions of this approach. One most easily acceptable to teachers and enjoying some vogue now is the school bookshop or, for younger children, toy fair and bookshop. On the school premises, it has an obvious benefit for children, but, if parents can be recruited severally and regularly, it can be advantageous. This, most teachers would agree, is an important curriculum area and, with parents involved in a kind of organising-cum-training role, much might be gained. The parents would, in effect, be coached in the business of the choice and usage of books or toys through their heavy engagement with the day-to-day running of the shop, plus joint child-parent 'seminars' on the subject.

This is but one example of how an existing school facility might be deployed for something akin to a child-parent project. Another might be under cover of using parents' hobbies and attributes, as several schools imaginatively do, for the delectation of small bands of children. A teacher could astutely utilise such experiences as the basis for discussion with parents on child development, teaching method, and so forth. By and large, a weekly contact of the kind proposed in this section should be regarded as the ideal.

This characterisation of the parent as a 'student' has led to a seminal and fascinating debate, as yet unresolved, among those concerned with parental education. There are those who argue that the parent should be offered parental education in the limited sense of how a child learns, so that he or she can be more supportive. For instance, by understanding modern maths, father may be more able to help his son with his sets of Cuisenaire rods. But there are others who argue for a freer connotation, claiming that the task should be to educate the parent for himself or herself, in the belief that a more liberal education is the finest investment for civilised parenthood.

Like the American Constitution, therefore, parental education is open to both a 'strict' and a 'loose' interpretation. On this latter basis, many schools have offered programmes of straightforward adult education to parents, with dressmaking, keep-fit, cookery and hairdressing probably being the premier demands. There is no doubt a massive call for non-formal, friendly groups such as this, away, if possible, from the protocol of registers and fees. The Russell Report on Adult Education hinted at this need and, naturally enough, the school which meets it enjoys the bonus of the parent feeling increasingly at ease in the school. Thus the educational is aligned with the social.

Although many primary schools have pioneered this technique with great spirit, this is one case where the secondary school, with its range of amenities and staffing, scores heavily. Often in association with the further education division of its authority, the secondary school can lay on an imposing schedule, although those that do so specifically with parents in mind are rare. What has caused considerable interest, and no little disquiet, have been those secondary schools which, apart from liberally making their facilities available to parents in afternoons or evenings and during holidays, have experimented with senior pupil-adult classes.

Given the distinction between the pre- and post-adolescent pupil with regard to parental-child contact, this would seem to be the equivalent of the child-parent project. In the primary school, the parent and their *own* children work together in duo or trio, learning as a family unit. In the senior echelons, the parents there move as citizens in their own right, and their togetherness with the pupils is more symbolic of home-school links than real. It also represents an important piece of thinking about the recognition of pupils, especially older pupils, as members themselves of the 'educative community', as putative citizens and young adults. The O level maths class of fourteen 16-year-olds, four housewives, half-a-dozen from the further education grades, three older men looking for enhanced career prospects and a couple of old-age pensioners — that is the class possibly of the not too distant future, and it is analogous with the child-parent project.

Like most debates, the 'strict' versus 'free' interpretation of parental education need not lead to exclusive answers. Parental education of the child-centred kind is possibly more for the primary school and more of a short-term solution, ensuring that the parent understands, however sketchily, what the school is attempting. Parental education of the citizen-centred kind is perhaps more for the secondary school and more of a long-term solution, pursued in the hope that eventually the whole general quality of parent skills will be spectacularly improved.

To attain that end, there will have to be millions more like the mother in a school with a very brisk and plentiful home-school programme, who recently announced: 'It'll end up with the children waiting for us to come out of school!'

CHAPTER 7

Parents' committees . . . and parents' rooms

There are two other areas of parental liaison for consideration, each of them concerned with a rather specialised activity requiring great commitment by teacher, parent or both. Because of the tenor of that dedication and because of their more formalised nature, rather than because of any intrinsic similarity, they are discussed together here. They are parent committees and parent management or governance and parents' rooms, and it is intended to offer some comments concerning each.

(A) PARENT COMMITTEES AND MANAGEMENTS

These will be examined only briefly, for this matter concerns the parent extensively and the teacher relatively marginally. However, the initiative usually comes from the school, either to establish some form of committee or association, or to obey the authority's directive to arrange the appointment of a manager or governor.

A thoroughgoing parents' association, or PTA, or any form of standard parent group, can be of sound advantage to a school, not least in terms of raising funds, arranging social functions, offering labour assistance at school events, doubling as a political pressure group should occasion demand, and so on. What the school — the head and teachers, perhaps in concert with the parents — must decide is whether a formal organisation is the answer or not. One must recall that the over-riding objective is the improved attainment on the children's part. A triumphant seizure of purported rights on the part of parents, which somehow leads to a deterioration in the standards, would be anti-educational. The only worthwhile product of better parental participation should be better pupil expectation.

I am sceptical enough to be bothered by some parents and parents' groups which see the winning of some technical political point as an end in itself, irrespective of its effect on the children's schooling. I am as cynical about teachers who somehow manage to use parents' associations as instruments of inhibition, who behind the smug proclamation of allowing a PTA can actively deploy it to stem any realistic dialogue. They are able shrewdly to gather any possible dissident or grumbling parents into one bag, and then tie the PTA knot tight round the neck of the sack.

There is also the question of group dynamics. Many of us in the home-school world have observed the phenomenon of a far from formal weekly meeting of mothers creating its own psychological barrier. It might be simple enough to persuade twenty to join a mothers' club enjoying a relaxed session together every Tuesday afternoon. Recruiting the twenty-first may be the problem, for the twenty-first may have to invade, emotionally speaking, the territory occupied by the original score. What in old-fashioned argot was called a clique often forms itself unconsciously: it is not that the twenty originals deliberately ostracise a willing novitiate: rather is it that, unwillingly, an infrastructure of conventions and values is developed, defended by those inside and threatening to those without.

When this is projected into the world of company law, with the large-scale PTAs with their committees, motions, minutes and resolutions, those conventions become ritualised. Particularly, in cultures where that council chamber conduct is alien, it has created and can create desperate communications problems. It is not simply a class matter, for – as has been exemplified in the first crop of parent managers – the trade unionist may be as happy and secure in the committee role as the business executive. Some schools have constructed parent committees, for instance, on the basis of one representative to every hundred families and the whole question is wide open for inexhaustible experiment.

It is simply a revamping of a central theme of this book that action should not be foreign to the life-style of the intended protagonists. If a school – teachers and parents – can honestly judge that it will be more fruitful to avoid formal structures, then that is fine, just as the reverse – the high-powered committee where the catchment culture demands – is equally valid.

Something of the same applies to parents being appointed as managers and governors of schools and, having served both as a co-operative secondary school governor and as parent manager in a primary school, I speak with feeling if not authority. I have, for some time, been a proponent of the view that a managing or governing board should have at least two managers, partly for cover in case of unavoidable absence, and partly to act as supports, the one for the other, in what might be an alien situation.

The school might do two things to help its parent managers or governors. One would be to offer some form of training in the style and management of the school and to give scope to the elected parent to build up an exact picture of how the school works. This could be done tactfully and without condescension, and most parent managers would probably welcome such an opportunity. The other would be to give the parent manager or governor absolute freedom to employ the school facilities for communicating with the parent body. This might be a regular column in the school's newsletter, or it might be the use of the school hall, with all the trimmings provided which the school would itself add. It might be appropriate to introduce the parent delegate into an existing round of school-parent occasions or to plan a pleasant social event with a talk by, or discussion led by, the elected parent at some point in the proceedings. One has been alarmed to learn of schools tacitly refusing parent governors this privilege.

My own view is that much of the necessarily formal side of home-school dialogue should, in future, be developed around the person of the school manager/governor, and that the school should really pull out the stops to make this important post viable, not to succour the elected parent as a person, but for the sake of the school's own communion with the homes it is serving.

Where permissible, I would be inclined carefully to examine the electoral mode adopted by a school. The straightforward postal nomination plus a polling session, or the meeting of parents with a show of hands or on-the-spot ballot, has so far produced rather impoverished results in many schools, especially when one bears in mind the quantity of parents who, up and down the country, have responded to rather more colourful approaches. Elections linked by 'class'-based parental nominees; postal or door-to-door voting; voting during some cheerful social gathering – all these may need to be tried in an effort to ensure maximum support for this new constitutional device, which, particularly in its infancy, is bound to be a little slow-moving.

(B) PARENTS' ROOMS

Older schools, with spare capacity, have developed parents' rooms, while newly designed schools have very occasionally included such an amenity, although the strictness of economics has tended to tell against this. What are they, in fact, for?

Simply, they offer the parents a niche of their own in the school where they can develop their own vocational, social or educational activities. It is, in a word, a clubroom. Several, with local authority help, have been amply furnished; one or two even boast a bar, usually for temperance but occasionally for more convivial beverages. Several include sewing machines and other items of domestic technology, so that parents can manufacture either garments or fabrics for themselves or for the school entertainment or play. Most allow the parents to decorate the room and choose fittings, curtains and furnishing, and they are used for meetings of one kind or another, and also on a regular basis for groups or even classes in various subjects.

They give the parent a physical stake in the school. They establish a 'third world', not quite of the school but yet again by no means remote from it. They bring the parent into intensely direct contact with the teacher, and yet somehow manage to keep the parent out of the teacher's hair. For schools with some capacity, they can be a fruitful investment, and several figure as the most attractive base in the building.

Their disadvantage is the same as most home-school activities. They can be used unscrupulously by the school to keep the parents out of harm's way or to prevent the parents from, in the argot of the unsympathetic school, 'interfering'. They do allow the superficially friendly but basically hostile headteacher to fasten up the parents in a kind of do-it-yourself penitentiary, all the while protesting that no one could be more helpful and progressive than he.

All in all, it is a brave step towards very direct dialogue for a school, fully and unequivocally, to offer its parents this facility. The brevity of the treatment should not be judged as measuring its import. Obviously, the sorts of rooms, the sorts of parents and the sorts of activities vary so remarkably that only the general principle can be enunciated. Where the authority is not keen to spend money, it may be over to the parents to beat up the wind. The parents' room, serving refreshments or acting as base for a bingo session or jumble sale, is immediately a vantage point for such fund-raising. The more fully the parents' room is thus taken over in its entirety by the parent body, the better the venture, in precept and in practice, for, above all, it offers the nearest to a neutral ground for the home-school match in a game where one side is normally doomed to play away and the other at home.

CHAPTER 8

The ultimate in home and school relations

To sustain the metaphor of the football match, the teacher is really confronted with an 'away' fixture when he or she decides to attempt home-visiting; the final foray into parental education, it reaches into the very heart of the child's social milieu and can easily be misinterpreted as a gross intervention into private life. Because of its intimacy, it polarises the whole issue of home and school relations. The parent is at home and there is a good chance of a totally relaxed atmosphere in which the most convincing teacher-parent dialogue may be attempted. Alternatively, the parent may feel, by that token of intimacy, prickly with embarrassment, leaving the teacher very vulnerable.

More than all other home-school enterprises, this is the one requiring most delicate handling. The suggestion that all teachers should home-visit is a recipe for discomfort and even embarrassment. The teacher must be positive that the welcome will be warm and that, indeed, the away match is a 'friendly'! Not all teachers can or should be confident of this, nor should they feel worried that it falls outside their ken. It is quite a specialised form of approach.

Successful home-visiting often arises spontaneously, when, for instance, a child or a message has to be delivered, and the conversation-piece in the home grows naturally. This is a proper opportunity, too, for the teacher to assess whether a regular home-visiting pattern is called for, either on the part of the parent or the teacher; or, for that matter, most critically the child, who stands to be chief beneficiary or otherwise. Naturally, a message bearing tidings of gloom and despondency about the child is rarely guaranteed to establish a cosy three- or foursome around the kitchen table. The skilful teacher, nevertheless, might utilise even bad news to devise an opening.

Another approach is to travel round parental residences with news of some extra-special school occasion, delivering a form of personal invitation. There can be some self-propulsion in this. One highly

competent and pioneer 'home-visitor' of my acquaintance found, after
two or three calls, that both children and parents were eagerly awaiting
her arrival, asking her when she was going to come to 'our home', and
evidently quite prepared to enjoy hurt feelings if she failed to do so.
Visits might arise, conversely, from events in school where the parents,
having been invited into the school, may be prevailed upon to return
the compliment and invite the teacher home. The pleasantest visiting is
the result of direct invitation by the parent.

But it is difficult to obtain the correct mixture of the informal and
the formal. There must be some formality, for the venture must have
nothing of the 'favourite son of a favourite son' (to borrow from
American politicking) about it to suggest that the teacher has chosen
cronies. I vividly recall my own junior school, where a child annually
invited home for tea his new teacher, both of them having to brave a
desultory barrage of 'duckies', as we referred in those parts to the small
stone missile. Like all other education selling, it should be above-board
in the sense of being seen to be done for a particular purpose as part of
the teacher's function.

A chatty letter to all parents, perhaps inviting *them* to invite *you* if
they so wished; a brief get-together with all parents to alert them to
what you have in mind — these would be ways of ensuring that the
exercise was regarded as an educational and not a social round.

Having gained ingress, the willing teacher might do best to canvass
what hints are available from the small troupe of educational visitors
now extant. According to Geoffrey Poulton, who has carefully
researched the field, there are now more than seventy full-time
educational visitors operating in England. These are normally working
in disadvantaged areas and several work in the pre-school field, for their
early provenance was during the Educational Priority Area projects
(1968—71) which, especially in the West Riding, emphasised the plight
of the under-5s. It was argued earlier that schools must decide how to
deploy staff *vis-à-vis* the home and whether, for instance, to request
one member of staff to bear the major brunt. Few schools, as yet, will
enjoy the luxury of an educational visitor to organise the main sector
of home-school relations and to undertake the home-visiting, but others
may feel it profitable to release a teacher for a goodly proportion of
time. In the secondary schools there is usually at present some format
of pastoral care, with several counsellors or other appointments
available for these functions.

About a year ago the 'Priority' organisation in Liverpool, of which I
have been Director and which has busied itself with a broad range of
parental education, drew up a paper on educational visiting.

I have decided to quote liberal extracts from this memorandum, so
that schools or teachers wishing to begin or develop home-visiting will

be able to select items of specific assistance. Whether this plays a large or tiny role in the school's programme, there may be something of interest in these quotations.

EDUCATIONAL VISITING

(A) AIMS OF THE EDUCATIONAL VISITOR

(1) To encourage and reinforce the parent in his/her educative role before the child starts school and throughout child's school life.
(2) To foster the partnership between home and school in all its aspects, including the recognition of the importance of the home as the initial and crucial educative influence.
(3) To develop an atmosphere in which the school welcomes and ventures out into the community.

(B) OBJECTIVES

It is important to bear in mind that the objectives of any Educational Visiting Programme will vary according to the needs of the school and its community.

(1) To encourage parents to see their role as educators, to give parents the techniques to fulfil the educative role of parenthood, and to foster a working partnership between parents and teachers to that end. Parents might require help to perceive the patterns of intellectual, social and emotional development of their children and encouragement to see the importance of their contributions to this process.
(2) To raise the level of educational awareness of a school's parent population.
(3) To introduce into the home of children who will eventually attend infants schools, ideas and materials which will encourage their pre-school conceptual, perceptual and motor development. Perhaps to monitor the progress of each child visited and develop with the parent individual programmes to match the child's needs and responses. In this respect it may be more necessary to identify those children who will not attend nursery classes or pre-school playgroups for specific attention.
(4) To develop existing links between home and school. To stimulate interest amongst parents in the school's curriculum. To encourage greater parental participation in all school activities. To support teachers in developing an interest in and understanding of the backgrounds and culture of the parents and children.

(5) To introduce and explain the use of educational materials in the home and to keep parents informed, at first hand, of books, games and other materials available for young children.

(6) To allow the child to develop an easy relationship with an educator and to develop confidence in an educational situation on his own territory, so reducing the anxiety which can accompany starting school, and to further facilitate transition from infant to junior school, junior to secondary school.

(7) To learn at first hand the difficulties experienced by families and where necessary to encourage parents to be aware of and take advantage of facilities offered by other existing social and educational agencies.

(8) To encourage the parents, children and teachers to view education as a continuous and joyful experience.

(C) METHOD

(1) It is important that before starting work in an area the Educational Visitor acquaints himself with other related agencies, and activities in the community. For example, the work of an Educational Welfare Officer, Social Worker and the situation of play groups etc. It is essential that the Educational Visitor be given a large measure of freedom to operate on a wider basis than one of close and limited contacts with a school and its children and parents. The Educational Visitor must offer an educational service to the community, rather than the school. The distinction is a fine one, but an important one. Activities which will benefit the school may be much more limited in value than those which will benefit the community generally and inevitably benefit the school.

(2) The Educational Visitor has a distinct professional role and should be accorded a sufficiently independent status in order to determine where his/her activities and help might be most needed and effective.

(3) There are two distinct operational levels for the educational visitor:
   (a) The specific operations of individual contacts and relationships with parents and children through home visiting.
   (b) The less specific operation of work on a more general community orientated basis.

(a) *Specific Operations*

(i) *Initial Visiting in the Home.* This could even take the form of a friendly invitation to participate in a venture that requires the skills and expertise of the parent as well as the teacher. However, while the objectives of visits are determined professionally by the Visitor, the method should be dictated by the wishes of parents.

It seems to us that the whole tone of the initial visit is crucial. Many parents may not see immediately or ultimately the implications of such participation. Early visits could very easily lapse into 'mothers rest' periods while the visitor home tutors the child. This may be an essential beginning, but the principal underlying aim is the involvement of parent and child, and therefore participation is more important than any activity.

(ii) *Subsequent Visiting.* Once involvement is achieved, a 'kit' of materials could be left in the home and parents encouraged to use it between visits. The kit could be more than a means of encouraging parent/child contact, and might be carefully and systematically arranged and introduced, so as to develop specific preselected skills.

It will be readily apparent that too much emphasis could be placed on such organisation. Differential abilities and rates of development of children would make close control of such a programmed kit difficult, but it seems to us a useful tool, particularly if learning resources that are readily available in the home (bean cans, kitchen sink, pots and pans, stairs) are fitted into a development pattern.

(b) *Non-Specific Visiting*
It is important to realise that to confine the Educational Visitor's activities to one-to-one situation home visits is to seriously limit his scope and therefore minimise his effectiveness.

(i) *Education Parties.* Following the example of 'Tupperware Parties' and many other commercial home selling techniques to groups in the home of a hostess, one visitor can address him/herself to groups of mums meeting rotationally in the homes of each other. Afternoon visits could be illustrated by children playing. Evening visits can be very productive in discussing problems (e.g. reading i.t.a./maths) and can be useful for their potential in involving fathers.

(ii) *Mothers' Groups.* It is as well to realise that the mother away from home in the evening, without her children, can re-charge her batteries. The house can be a tying place, and the Educational Visitor should always be alive to the possibility and potentiality of the introduction of wider adult educational provision. The more complete people the parents are, the more productive will be any involvement with the child that is propagated.

(iii) *Playgroups.* Whether based in a school, or outside the school and unrelated to it, the pre-school playgroup movement is one to which the Visitor could profitably attach himself. The support and extension of the movement is a valuable end in itself, apart from which, attachment to a playgroup would give ready contact with mothers on a group basis.

We have had some success with the setting up of co-operatively managed playgroups on school premises, where mothers run the playgroup for their own children on a rota basis. Such a scheme is basic stock in trade for the Visitor trying to increase the educational awareness of any group.

(iv) *School Groups.* As with mother groups, the home visiting can be extended into involvement of parents, teachers and staff, in school hours, during the evening, in adult groups, classroom activities or involvement of parents in curriculum work or planning. The Educational Visitor should aim to place home/school relationships on such a basis that home visiting in individual cases becomes less and less necessary.

(v) *School Projection.* There is no point in an Educational Visitor in isolation taking educational information and advice and support to parents. The school must play its major part. Therefore another aspect of the Educational Visitor's work is to encourage the school to project itself into the community in which the Educational Visitor is working. By such simple techniques as the display of school work in shops, pubs, on street corners, the Educational Visitor can circulate outside the school in an educational atmosphere.

(D) MATERIALS

(1)   In direct consequence to this last sentence, initiative and resourcefulness are called for to take every opportunity to utilise and encourage the mother to use such materials and ideas that are in the home already, in a more directly 'educative' sense. The crucial factor about materials is that it is not what a child has, but what it does with them, that is important. The Educational Visitor is in a unique position to recognise the potentiality of materials and ideas in and around the home, that would otherwise lie unused and unconsidered.

(2)   Notwithstanding this, it does seem a part of the Visitor's function to carry into the home ideas about the suitability and potentiality of commercially produced materials. A stock of demonstration equipment, much of it expendable, is essential, and financial support should allow for this.

To illustrate this very simply; the most commonly bought type of painting equipment we have found is the tin-boxed, palette type, six hair-bristle brushes, with paints reacting to water rather in the form of pre-stressed concrete. Three-year-olds can't paint with this. We can't. It becomes the function of the Visitor to introduce powder/palette/ready mixed/non-spill/finger paints; a variety of brushes up to the half-inch door brush. It becomes also the function of the Visitor to show parents how to use them.

(3) Every opportunity should be taken to encourage parents to make apparatus with the Visitor's help. The making of equipment, particularly large items such as dolls' houses and puppet theatres, can be a means of surmounting one of the more difficult problems that will be encountered, that of involving fathers.

(4) The importance of a child's linguistic abilities in relation to his future performance must be recognised by the Educational Visitor. The Educational Visitor should be aware of opportunities within the home to extend the child's language and should encourage parents to talk to their children. It may be necessary to be quite specific as to what words should be introduced in certain situations, e.g. 'float', 'sink', 'splash' could be introduced at bath-time. The Educational Visitor should be aiming throughout to increase the linguistic interaction between parent and child.

The ultimate objective is not just to raise individual attainments and awareness, but to lift the overall educational awareness of community.

(i) *Staff Liaison*. The Educational Visitor must become an accepted member of the school staff and must be as frequent and welcome a presence in the staffroom, and the headmaster's room, as he is in homes.

He should always serve as a reminder to the school that the educative process, however it is defined, can only be fully effective when orientated towards the family as a whole rather than the individual child in the classroom.

(E) ADDITIONAL ASPECTS

(1) *Time of Visits*

The Educational Visitor must be prepared to visit at any time, and therefore should be given the responsibility and flexibility of working conditions to arrange this. *Some* evening and *some* weekend visiting and work is essential and inevitable if all potential beneficiaries are to be contacted.

(2) *Records*

We make the point that the Visitor will find himself at the nexus of a complex set of relationships between head/staff/parent and child. He will find himself needing to exercise a measure of responsibility in accordance with the confidential and sensitive nature of the relationships made. Thus narrative records of the more traditional kind could easily become extremely inhibitive and of limited use.

It is recommended that whatever records are kept should be in the nature of a chart for development, incorporating both parental contribution and Educational Visitor's observation. This idea of a co-operative and open record enables a more positive building on strengths rather than collating of weakness and is perhaps one of the more exciting ideas we have to offer.

(3) *Situation*

Although he is a member of the school(s) staff, and although preparation of a programme should involve the head(s) and staff(s) in question it must be borne in mind that the Educational Visitor might well work with a group of schools. Therefore, the Visitor's situation within the educational hierarchy must be defined, even if it be one of harmonious independence.

(4) *Age-Range*

The need is seen for an initial and particular emphasis on pre-school work, as this is the age at which children are closest to their parents and the age at which the parent is most approachable about the child and most susceptible to involvement.

Children in this age-range will in a remarkably short period of time make up the school population but even where initial contacts are made with pre-school children, those children will have older siblings in school.

A wide range of contacts will quickly emerge. It might be restrictive to confine the activities of the Visitor to one highly specific group, e.g. the next term's intake, remedial group, known social problems.

The building up of pre-school provision and liaison with existing and growing provision will also concern the Educational Visitor.

(5) *Travelling Allowances*

Rapid mobility is essential. The Educational Visitor is a traveller, and travelling time is not work time. The Educational Visitor also needs to carry round materials that can grow to large proportions even though individual items may be small.

A car allowance is therefore essential, and an appropriate running allowance should be considered.

The Educational Visitor should be adaptable and sensitive. There is the need to be able to communicate meaningfully across a wide range of personnel, officers, attitudes, personalities.

It seems that the Educational Visitor should be a qualified and experienced teacher, who has had the widest practical experience of a wide range of educational ideas, techniques and equipment. Some insights into the experience of educational testing and evaluative techniques would be a useful acquisition. The Educational Visitor must be committed to the idea that environment exerts an enormous influence on educability. It is perhaps suggested that some intensive and detailed inquiry into the determinants of educability etc. form part of any training programme, even of an 'in service' nature.

I am indebted to colleagues Bill Thurston, Sheila Cronin, Susan Bell, Celia Burn and others for their tidy and competent authorship of this hitherto unpublished paper. It summarises neatly many of the propositions made during the later sections of this book, as well as introducing certain new and penetrating issues, such as the question of travelling allowance, records and materials. The issue of mobility needs to be covered and, as with all teaching, the maintenance of thorough records, not least because of the need for continuity with changes of staff, and so on, is indispensable.

Above all, the paper makes clear the absolute essence of home-visiting. It must have the object of improving the child's education through his parents' augmented capacity and it must be regular. A school may be only able to do a little but, even so, it must not be casual. It must be a planned and co-ordinated strategy, often with some form of kit. The emphasis in their paper is always practical: it is always advising on *active* participation on the part of parents and upon giving their children and themselves tasks to accomplish. It is far from the friendly but inconsequential fireside chat over a pot of tea.

The paper on educational visiting reminds us of a point made at the outset that home-school relations should not be confused with other professional ideas like that of the educational welfare officer. Apart from the principle involved in that distinction, it is, quite obviously, sound and tactful diplomacy.

A full account of home or educational visiting has been necessary because, in reversing the entire question of education, it very much underlines the significance of educational salesmanship. It presses the thesis that the home is, if anything, more compelling an influence than the school and, at least geographically, home-visiting turns educational teaching on its head. In a phrase, it takes the classroom to the doorstep. It is the ultimate in home and school relations.

CHAPTER 9

Tried mechanics

A final chapter in the series of home-school activities is devoted to one or two practical excerpts, in an effort to recall that one is offering tried mechanics and not nebulous thoughts.

(A) SCHOOLS' ACTIVITIES DURING 'SUPPORT OUR SCHOOLS' WEEK

This list was assembled from a number of schools which, during a given week, attempted to attract as many parents into their schools as possible. It gives some indication of the variety of items without teachers doing anything radically 'daring'.

1 'At Home' – exhibition of schoolwork and turns by children
2 Disco by mums and staff (usually weekly event)
3 'Spring Fair' – organised by parents
4 Grand Opening of Parents' Room
5 Visit to large park for various activities with parents and children
6 Play for parents and children by visiting company
7 Arts and crafts exhibition (including parents' work)
8 Five-a-side football competition between schools
9 Open House – parents' evening with entertainment
10 Fancy dress event, including 'family' entries
11 Exhibition of children's work for parents
12 Infants' performance of music etc. for parents
13 Parade by infants to welcome 'Home-School Harry'
14 Film show for parents and children
15 Open night with entertainment specially provided
16 Police safety demonstration with parents invited to take part
17 Sports day with parents' events and parents' help
18 'Harry's Hat Parade' – parents and children in 'fancy hat' competition
19 Parents' afternoons on a class basis, each day of week
20 'Liverpool Sounds' – concert and musical (three shows for parents)
21 Morning assembly (with parents assisting in reading etc.)

22 Creative display of junior dance, music, gymnastics and drama
23 Cabaret — parent/teacher social, with parent/teacher performance
24 Musical request programme — children doing parents' 'requests'
25 Open day — concert and coffee for parents, plus visits to class-bases
26 Party for parents who had helped during year given by children
27 Outing to theatre — parents, staff and pupils
28 Nursery picnic, with parents invited to accompany the outing
29 Beauty evening and fashion parade for mothers
30 International food tasting evening — in a multiracial school
31 World Children's Day Festival Pageant — in a multiracial school
32 Evening trip for parents to recreation or commercial spots
33 Mothers' afternoon — help create frieze or collage or other piece of
   work for school

(B) ONE INFANTS SCHOOL'S ACTIVITIES DURING 'SUPPORT OUR
   SCHOOLS' WEEK

Harry's tea-party for grandparents/OAPs etc.
Book sales
Art exhibitions
Visit to Chester (two classes)
Coffee mornings
Parents' day — slides and talk
Morning services with parents
Open day games
Trip to Ffrith Beach
Alice in Wonderland (students' performance for parents and children)
Bring-and-buy sale, opened by Harry
Visits to local parks
Fancy dress
'At Home'
Prize-giving and sports afternoon
Swimming with parents
Dressmaking
Football
Arts workshop
Community class
Opening of parent/child library
Exhibition of environmental studies
Five-a-side football
Maths with parents
Cabaret — mums' and dads' night out
Ladies' football match 'Shankley v. Bingham'
Film — tour of the parish

Open air mini-sports
Nursery entertainment
Presentation of 'Castle' to Harry, and Everton toffees by Mother
    Noblett
Walk through the 'Squares'
Church service with parents
Old Time Music Hall for OAPs
Children's party
Visit to Ainsdale
Visit to Clarke Gardens
Schools' music festival
Open week

(C) ONE TEACHER'S VIEW OF A YEAR'S WORK ON THE HOME/SCHOOL
    FRONT

A Merseyside teacher kindly consented to catalogue all she had
accomplished on the home/school front during the school year. The
teacher is, admittedly, an experienced 'home-schooler', but this log is
not, by the standards of several teachers, including this one,
exceptional. It does give some guide to what might be managed with
foresight, invention and planning.

1 Display board – pupils' own work for parents to see
2 One or two parents to stay to school dinner on a regular basis
3 See people by appointment
4 Sewing mornings, e.g. dressing-up box and mending or making
   aprons
5 Projects, e.g. inquiry into neighbourhood elderly sick, with help
   from parents
6 Clothing supply – mothers responsible for thrift box occasionally
   on Friday mornings
7 Child care talks – teeth, hair, minor injuries, books, toys, diet,
   clothing especially shoes; experts give fifteen-minute talks, with
   parents in attendance
8 Indoor gardens – improve parents' room and give interest which
   might carry over to home
9 Dressmaking, knitting, crochet and cookery groups
10 Visits – both teacher for homes and teacher on outings with parent
   groups
11 Newsletter for parents with parental contributions
12 Evening meeting of parents
13 Games on school lawn – children and parents
14 Parents' room available always – mothers responsible for its fabric
   and maintenance

It might be added that most of these activities were focused on the parents' room known, in this case, very validly, as 'The Parents' Workshop'.

(D) TEN COMMANDMENTS FOR THE EXHIBITION OF WORK IN SHOPS

(1) *Make sure*
(a) *That when you go* to ask for work to be put up, you take 'samples' with you. This puts the shopkeeper in the picture, so that he knows exactly what he is letting himself in for.
(b) Don't be put off, because they won't all say 'yes' first time.
(c) Samples help them say 'yes', but if you want near 100 per cent co-operation, take three or four small children with you, each carrying his own work!

(2) *Make sure*
(a) *You invite all shops to participate.* If you miss some out, they will complain later about the 'free advertising' that the others are getting: 'Why didn't they ask us, is it because we are Catholics?' said one Liverpool butcher.

(3) *Make sure*
(a) *That you spy out the land.* When you go to put work up, make a strict appointment with the shopkeeper and be on time. Suggest to him a time of day when he is not too busy.
(b) Be quick when putting work up. In and out. Go back later, on your own, to talk about the work.
(c) Ask him to help you put the work up — especially if there is any ladder climbing to do. He will be used to it and insured, while you may be neither.
(d) Assess the available space, and take only such work as fits into that space allocated by the shopkeeper. Good relations can be ruined by *ad hoc* negotiations for another bit of wall.

(4) *Make sure*
(a) *You take the kids with you* when you take work to the shops. It is their work anyway.
(b) But you should have another adult to watch them outside while you are inside with a small group of helpers — (parents?).

(5) *Make sure*
(a) *You explain what it is all about*
(b) Clear, concise headings to each piece of work:
      e.g. 'Collage by 8-year-olds'.

(c) Explain also what you are aiming at:
    e.g. 'Collage is ... We do it because ...'.
(d) 'Translations' of i.t.a. and infant spelling aberrations can be helpful and informative.

(6) *Make sure*
(a) *You are prepared for mounting difficulties.*
(b) The work to go up should be mounted on its backing in advance, and suitably sized for the available space.
(c) Cow gum neither leaves marks on walls, nor does it rip paper. 'Bluetack' is similarly successful. Sellotape can lead to ripped paper in a draughty spot, and while the County Architect and Clerk of Works are fair game, shopkeepers don't like their paint coming away from the walls when you take work down.
(d) Watch tiled surfaces in steamy chippies and smelly fish shops. The shopkeeper needs to clean them often, and nothing except grease will stick to smooth tiles anyway.

(7) *Make sure*
(a) *You evaluate.* Ask the shopkeeper what he thinks, ask him what his customers have said. Take the trouble, and make the time, to explain to him what is behind the work that goes up in his shop (aims, objectives, techniques and all); you then have the perfect home-school PR man.

(8) *Make sure*
(a) *You are always on the lookout for other display places.* Doctors' and dentists' waiting-rooms − pubs − buses − advertising hoardings lying fallow.

(9) *Make sure*
    Your work is suitable to the location in which it is displayed; e.g.
(a) How far away the spectator is likely to be will determine the type of work to go up (written or visual − fine line or broad brush art work).
(b) How long the spectator is likely to stay will have a similar effect (stories go down well in the pub, as does poetry, where people spend long, otherwise boring hours therein).
(c) Try not to cause obstructions to the shop's work (supermarket check-out clerks can be driven to apoplexy by the admiring reader of creative English at 7.30 in a Friday night rush hour!).
(d) School magazines, newsletters, class newspapers, compete very well with two-year-old *Reader's Digests* in the waiting-room or hairdresser's.

(10) *Make sure*
There is some point to it, by combining variety with structure, for
example:
(a) First display the results of a local 'shopping survey'.
(b) Second, an appropriate project, e.g. fishing, what we eat, the
Argentinian cowboy, our teeth, the human body, in the obviously
appropriate situation.
(c) Then get clever. The treatment of an identical theme by each class
in the school to show the differing approaches at each age-range.

Thus you can be structured and informative.
And always invite them back, by the shopkeepers and people in the
community writing for your magazine, visiting you in turn, etc.

(E) TEN COMMANDMENTS FOR THE DO-IT-YOURSELF PROCESSION ORGANISER

First the Adults
(1) *Keep them happy.* Whenever you undertake something that
disrupts routine, whether it is an open day, a school play or a
procession, people are under stress. Not the children! They will be
well balanced. But the parents and teachers, they are the neurotics
of such situations.
Keep them smiling. It is soon over, and invariably any corporate
effort will bring you all closer together.
(2) *Keep them informed.* Make sure everybody knows why you are
processing. The whole point is to express your belief in something,
even if you just want to say:

'WE LIKE SCHOOL!'

So: (a) Make sure your parents know what you are doing, when
and why (letters, talks, posters around the school).
(b) Make sure the community knows what you are doing,
when and why (posters in shops, advertisements on the
outside of the school building, local press, banners and
slogans on the day, a catchphrase or 'logo').
(3) *Keep them involved.* Parents can be a lot of help in labour-intensive
situations such as preparing for processions, either on the day, or
beforehand, with costumes etc.

Next the Children
(4) *Keep them excited.* Yes, you read that correctly. The sound of a
distant, but approaching brass band still excites me! Don't dampen
enthusiasm too much, it's a procession, not a maths test.

    (a) Dress up: but make sure your hats (elf-hats, red Indian feathers, cowboy hats, United Nations hats etc.) stay on in the winds that *always* blow on procession days.

    (b) Flimsies and lace can be very cold, even in summer. Simple but substantial costume is best, probably as additions to normal school clothes.

    (c) Have a theme (religious, harvest, state occasions, birthdays and anniversaries, we like school).

(5) *Keep them safe*

    (a) You must tell the police! They will be very helpful with traffic, just find the most local station in the telephone book.

    (b) The school lollipop *person* is invaluable. Worth a few bob from the school fund.

    (c) Keep off main roads.

    (d) Try to turn *left* as often as possible, it is much safer than turning right.

    (e) Noise (e.g. the band, or public address system) is as valuable as a safety feature as it is as a publicity feature. At least the motorist knows *something* is around the corner.

(6) *Keep them in order*

    (a) Walking behind some sort of 'figurehead' is useful. This can be a child in costume, a banner, a band, or just a car.

    (b) Sources of bands: the Police Band, 'Irish Clubs', 'Pipe Bands', Works 'Silver Bands', Secondary School Bands, Scouts, Boys' Brigade.

    (c) Try a public address system with taped music and microphone. They must do *something* between elections!

    (d) Try decorating PE hoops and making the children hold on to them in fours.

    (e) Hanging on to streamers from an old yard-brush pole is another decorative and effective way of stopping them from wandering.

    (f) Very young children (under 5) might walk better with mum holding their hand.

    (g) Begin the procession with once round the playground, then they are all in order by the time you get on to the road.

(7) *Keep them busy*

    (a) Everyone should have a streamer to stream, and waver to wave, a shaker to shake, or a banner to . . .

    (b) Lots of banners, preferably made by the children themselves beforehand. 'Done it myself' is best.

    (c) Little arms get tired quickly, even if they are holding something light. Give them all a turn at the big things — keep the peace as well as keep them fresh.

(8) *Keep them in sections.* Remember your O level physics? Sound takes time to travel, and even the back of the Grenadier Guards has trouble marching in time to the band. Don't try to sing all together.
  (a) Keep in groups, walk in groups, sing in groups, each supervised individually.
  (b) Have a programme of four or five songs which each group goes through as it wants, and practise them beforehand.
  (c) Simple songs. Make up your own words to well-known tunes, e.g. 'John Brown's Body':

> 'Our headmaster is the greatest in the land . . .'

  (d) Action and dancing songs are best,
      e.g. 'If you like our school clap your hands . . .'
      to the tune of 'She'll be coming round the mountain'. Keeps them warm this, too!
(9) *Keep them fresh*
(a) Depends on age of children, but roughly half an hour is plenty long enough for a school procession.
(b) Juniors may last longer.
(c) For under-5s, once round the school at the most.
(d) Practise the timing and distance yourself beforehand. There is no more depressing sight than a tired and bored procession.

And Finally Yourself
(10) *Be professional.* Behind every happy, fun-loving, informal procession, there is a sergeant-major with a stop watch and a clip board. Have a 'gauleiter', but keep him out of sight, so he doesn't stop you doing what you are out to do, which is to have fun and enjoy yourself.

NB I am grateful to Bill Thurston of the Liverpool Home-School Development Unit for preparing, in a kind of out-Moseying Moses mood, these twenty commandments.

newhere a watershed is reached and passed.
reasonably healthy and enthusiastic regard
a pleasant byway of teaching from a full
f educational salesmanship for parents in a

t the teacher's professional persona changes
at has been termed, borrowing from our PE
This is a case of the teacher adapting a
ahead, in a futuristic manner, to a time
as a social as well as an academic figure. It
re like the general practitioner, as the
'educative community' being served. It is
tive community, that is, the totality of
dly and dynamically for the pupil's
pt of community automatically seen in a
nse. For some pupils in some schools there
erlay of the residential upon the educative
' be of advantage. In some schools — the
ary in a fragmented or oddly located
e so. In any event, however tight the
ical or political catchment of the school,
eeding into the educative community. One
elevision or advertising pop music.
role would be; but its geographical progress
r direction. Simply, it would be topsy-turvy.
would turn the traditional teacher-role upon
ould be concerned with child and parent *in*
d not, incidentally, just with parent. It is the
portant. Moreover, the teachers would relate
ty than they have previously embraced,
the narrow pale of the school within which
constrained. Another way of saying this is
ll become adult educationists as well as
t the borders of their work-pattern will be
factors determining the children's
remain perhaps the focus or the
the enterprise, but it will cease to be
only agency where education can be sought

f all, this growth of teachers into, so to
would create a spectacular change in the

cal propositions made in these pages relate
e teacher would be more effective for

PART THREE: WHERE NOW?
A FORWARD ROLE

Two years ago I did an open-air 'educational queries' radio broadcast at a holiday camp, and I was almost pushed into the swimming pool by an irate Bolton housewife who was worried about vertical grouping. Reading between the lines of the conversation, it appeared that the school her children attended was an efficient enough one, except for one flaw. It had never explained, once and over again, to this rightly angry Boltonian, the mysteries of what it was doing.

At its brightest and best, the English primary school is a fine product, arguably the best buy on the social services mart. Yet, time and again, we waste it through poor public relations. The school in Bolton had not sold itself to its parents and, apart from its public image, all we now understand of home influence on education might indicate that, through not selling, the very educational achievement of what ostensibly was a splendid school would be endangered. This is the lesson and the test of home-school relations: it is about preserving and improving educational attainment.

One continually hears tit-bits of parental conversation, such as:

'He just seems to play all day!'
'She doesn't know her tables yet.'
'You should see his spelling.'
'There's not the same discipline . . .'
'They let them do what they like there.'
'You weren't watching the telly again, were you?'

Providing (it's a massive 'providing') that the school's work is rationally organised, such talk suggests that the school's public relations machinery is in need of overhaul. Occasionally one hears teachers being dismissive of parents who grow uptight over vertical grouping or Cuisenaire rods. They even accuse parents of 'ignorance'. But unless the professional teacher is prepared to explain the school's tactics and methods, then little else can be expected. It is not only, we should recollect, the lack of reinforcement in the home for what the school offers; it is the hazard of that offering being contradicted or maimed. And, yet again, it must be emphasised that most parents are highly motivated with regard to their children's education: probably the interest in education among parents from all walks of life has never been greater.

Teachers have been their own worst enemies in terms of public relations. They have been dangerously reticent and shown a prim schoolmarmishness about revealing all to the citizenry. It must be repeated that this is one factor in the continuing inequality of educational attainment as related to social origins. And it must once more be stressed that this is not just an affliction borne by the lowest echelons of society. University entrance still remains the *summum bonum* of our educational hierarchy and a fair indicator of educational success and its attendant effect on life-chances.

The preparations of the various socio-occupational groups, born 1930–49, who have reached university is, according to the Nuffield College, Oxford, population mobility study, as follows (to the nearest percentage):

Professional and administrative, managerial	23 per cent
Inspectoral, supervisory, non-manual	8 per cent
Skilled manual	4 per cent
Semi-skilled and unskilled manual	2 per cent

Although the chances of children from the lower-working classes remain abysmally low, the upper-working class fare not much better, and even the lower-middle class look a little sick compared with the upper middles. Something like 7 per cent of the age-grouping finish up at university and thus the lower-middle class only hold their own with the national norm. Indeed, if equal numbers of each of the four groups were inspected, the professional group would contribute over one and a half times *more* university graduates than the rest combined!

As it is, that upper-class band, almost a quarter of whom go up to university, constitute only 10 or 11 per cent of the population; that is, 5 million people of whom $1\frac{1}{4}$ million have been to, are at or will go to, university. Arguably, the other 45 million or so of the populace are disadvantaged as against these 10 per cent-ers.

I offer these statistics to explain why parental education is necessary over practically the full gamut of the population, and is not just, so to speak, for the poor. Granted, much of the pioneer work has, rightly, been done, in what are now called Social Priority Areas. It is true that the emphasis there needs not only to be different but firmer than elsewhere. But educational salesmanship is a skill for all teachers in all schools.

Advertising may be regarded as meretricious by some puritanical teachers, and, of course, they are right to be critical of its excesses. But why, to paraphrase the Salvationist, Booth, should the devil have all the

quantity is augmented, so
The watershed separates a
for home-school liaison as
commitment to the issue
much more total setting.

It is at this juncture th
radically. It constitutes w
confrères, 'a forward role
progressive stance, lookin
when the teacher is viewe
sees the teacher, rather m
educational steward of th
stressed that it is the *educ
influences contributing fl
education; it is not a cond
physical or geographical s
may be a high degree of o
communities, and that ma
large secondary or the pri
situation — this might not
boundaries of the geograp
there are other influences
thinks of 'universals' like

Forward-looking such a
would also move in anoth
Taken to the ultimate, thi
its head. For the teacher v
duo, not just with child ar
composite unit which is in
to a wider breadth of soci
much broader, that is, tha
they have previously been
that teachers will possibly
child educationists, and th
dictated rather more by tl
education. The school will
headquarters or the hub o
regarded exclusively as the
or preferred.

Perhaps most dramatic
speak, 'social academician
'style' of education.

In many ways the prac
to this. They assume that

becoming an outgoing, inventive and colourful extrovert. This does not mean always noise and clamour; several successful home-schoolers have been quiet, restrained and superficially diffident. But they have been assured, personable and, operating according to the dictates of their personality traits, they have created a presence and a positive image for education. What it entails is a willingness to sell education for education's sake and to adapt a stance of verve and good cheer rather than of austerity.

It has frequently been salutary to discuss with the executives of holiday camps, supermarkets or similar places the question of education and public relations. Sometimes they show a marked reluctance to become involved on the grounds that, whereas they are engaged in gay and tempting ventures, education is grey and arid. It has been depressing to be told so often that education is bad for someone else's image. It is viewed so *separately* by too many of the public. Too rarely is it accepted as an aspect of ordinary life.

The yardstick of success in this suggested change of style would be the extent to which education and 'life' could be interwoven.

That is why a character of 'normalcy' in home-school relations has been underlined. It is about education being more like everything else. It is about education being a little more familiar to people and people feeling a little more comfortable with education. This is the reason that there have been descriptions of noticeboards and sign-posts, like a department store, or publications, like a magazine or a commercial company's letter, or exhibitions and parades according to the norms of the parent clientele, or of functions similarly assessed, whether discos or debates.

There have been suggestions about how education might merge with, and become a noticeable but not separate aspect of, the local subculture. It is about evoking an atmosphere in which education is a spontaneous conversation-piece in pubs, shops or wherever else. It is about chatting, in informed fashion, about education in whatever situation people naturally forgather.

Of course, eventually, the government and local authorities would have to recognise this shift in the meanings of how an educational service should perform. From the purely teaching point of view, two long-term reforms are essential. One is a vast reform of teacher education, pre-service and in-service, so that the teacher is prepared for a new job-orientation. This means changes in the context and the structure of courses and that requires a study in itself.

The other is conditions of service. My own hope would be that, rather than a dilution of professionalism, the teacher's status — and thus salary — would be bettered by this elevation in role. Nothing would be more guaranteed to place teachers on a par with lawyers or doctors than this ideal of them supervising the whole educational needs of the community. It would mean different hours – perhaps working ten sessions of a fifteen-sessions (morning, afternoon and evening periods) week. It might mean a different concept of the school holiday; the point being that the evening, the weekend and the holiday are still times when education, in this wider connotation, is proceeding. Just as one looks for education to gell more closely with shops, the workplace, the transport and leisure systems and other commonplace branches of 'life', so would one expect education and the holiday to come nearer together.

One must be careful to add that this does not envisage any savage pressure on teachers and their hours. All must be negotiated cautiously and fully and, heaven knows, many teachers answer unlimited calls on their time. But the act of 'professionalising' the selling of education to the community through schemes of parental education should require properly calculated contractual agreements about time, training, skills, salary and validly evaluated results. In brief, for a fully organised programme of this kind, it would mean teachers working perhaps a forty-hour or forty-five-hour week over possibly a forty-four-week year, but with the timetable of hours in the day, days in the week and weeks in the year monitored to ensure maximum coverage.

Although this view of the teacher as a kind of educational bailiff or convenor for the host community implies some eventual responsibility among ordinary citizens for education (in the same way, as was previously agreed, they accept some 'health' chores), it is probably true to envisage some increase in the teacher workforce. To meet the demands both of longer-run times and of new functions apropos the citizenship, there would need to be some augmentation in teacher numbers and thus this time of static or falling pupil populations might be an apposite moment to consider this fundamental question of role.

It would be the ultimate in the work of the new-style teacher if, when people met and said 'How are you?' or 'How do you do?' the question were intended educationally as well as medically. When we discuss our education with the same *élan* as we discuss our weather, our health, our relationships, our holidays, our motorcars, our football teams, our jobs, and so on, then a major step will have been taken towards the equalising of educational opportunities. For the very climate of the 'educative community' in which each child exists is one – not the sole, but one – crucial element in how well (or how badly) he or she manages at school. The higher and the more equal the quality of that climate, the better the chances for everyone. There is, first and last, therefore, a moral reason for placing education on sale.

Epilogue: Albert and His Schooling
(With sincere apologies to Marriott Edgar)

There's a famous occasion for parents, that's noted for hot air and fun,
And Mr and Mrs Ramsbottom went there with young Albert, their son.
The event it were called 'open evening', the place were the local sec.
mod.
The weather was fine, the evening was dry, but Albert were feeling
quite odd.
'Twere the night when it had to be stated what he'd do in this final
two years;
And as he'd done nowt in the first three, you could see why he'd
flurries and fears.
The school was a big one, but ancient; Ma had gone there herself as a
lass,
And the one that she'd had from her husband was the nearest she'd had
to a pass.
'We never thought much on exams,' said father to Albert, quite curt.
'Though your mother, when she were in t'fourth form, was commonly
known as School Cert.'
So into the school-hall they mustered; the Ramsbottoms remembered
each patch,
Though the stains on the walls were more filthy, with the drawings in
t'toilets to match.
The headmaster spoke of the prospects for children on passing exams;
And how t'others got t'rough end of stick like; and were led to the
slaughter like lambs.
He explained that each single O level would ensure that your wage-
packet rose;
Said mother to Albert, 'If he means what he says, tell him we'll take ten
of those.'
He spoke of the problems of GCE, and what the CSE might mean;
Ma muttered to Albert, 'I thought that those were honours y'got from
the Queen.'
Then they broke into groups with a teacher apiece, to talk over each
case, calm and mild,
And what timetable choices were open, per subject, per exam, per
child.
Albert's form-teacher he shook his head hard, and over his papers he
pored;
When he spoke of 'grade three' Pa felt he was back at his army medical
board.
'What about ROSLA, Albert?' he asked, which caused quite a nasty
to-do;

He said, 'It's cigarette papers, or the name of the Queen of Peru.'

'Nay lad,' said his teacher, gentle but firm, 'you must think about work pretty smart';

Said Ma, 'Pa's not thought of it these twenty years, d'you really think Albert might start?'

'It's a question of "options",' the teacher explained; said Ma 'What, it's t'do wi' his eyes?'

'No, it's choosing the subjects he's best at,' he said, 'and picking a course to his size.

'Come Albert,' the teacher continued, 'speak up, without favour or fear.'

'If I only did t'subjects I'm good at,' said Albert, 'I'd best just go home for the year.'

'What about th' arts?' asked the teacher, 'that's history and English and such,

Or what d'you reckon to science and maths?' 'Not much,' said young Albert, 'not much.'

'Come, come,' said the teacher, a trifle more stern, 'you'll just have to think something up.'

Said Mr Ramsbottom, 'Have you got GCEs on how Oldham might fare in the cup?

'He'd get a grade one for his whippets, and his pigeons you'd have to applaud.'

Said the teacher, 'That's never taken by our Regional Examining Board.'

'What good's all this schooling?' asked father, 'he'll end up in the mill, sure as fate,

'And the foreman's not likely to ask him what happened in 1708.'

'Have you no ambition, young Albert?' said the teacher, growing more cool.

'Aye,' said the lad, all excited, 'it's ruddy well leaving yon school.'

'Oh dear,' replied t'teacher, 'is there *no* course for which you would like to affirm?'

Pa said, 'Haydock Park is the course that we like, especially when t'going is firm.'

The teacher and family to differ agreed, without rights being sorted from wrongs,

'Twere a case of parties discussing t'same point, but speaking in two separate tongues.

Both were to blame — the school found no way of speaking up early and clear,

While Mr and Mrs Ramsbottom had just left it for owt to appear.

They'd both left it late, and neither could tell what t'other were trying to say.

The victim was Albert: he went straight into t'mill and that's where he is to this day.

For all that his schooling had done him, he might just as well have gone through

To be swallowed up whole by the lion on his visit to Blackpool Tower Zoo.

Bibliography

This is a brief bibliography of some books which are informative or influential in the home-school field. It is not an exhaustive list; perhaps it is even an eccentric one. It is intended to serve as a catalogue for consideration by a school intending to establish a small 'staff' reference library in this field from books of reasonably recent vintage.

C. and M. Ball, *Education for a Change* (Penguin, 1973).
P. Clyne, *The Disadvantaged Adult* (Longman, 1972).
D. H. Cohen, *The Learning Child* (Wildwood House, 1973).
M. Craft, J. Raynor and L. Cohen, *Linking Home and School* (Longman, 1967).
J. W. B. Douglas, *The Home and the School* (MacGibbon & Kee, 1964).
E. Goodacre, *Home and School Relations* (Home and School Council, 1968).
E. Goodacre, *School and Home* (NFER, 1970).
B. and R. Gross, *Radical School Reform* (Pelican, 1972; first published 1969).
H. Kohl, *Reading, How to* (Penguin, 1974).
V. Houghton and K. Richardson, *Recurrent Education* (Ward Lock, 1974).
T. Lovett, *Adult Education, Community Development and the Working Class* (Ward Lock, 1975).
P. McGeeney, *Parents are Welcome* (Longman, 1967).
E. Midwinter, *Social Environment and the Urban School* (Ward Lock, 1972).
E. Midwinter, *Priority Education* (Penguin, 1972).
C. Mitchell, *Time for School* (Penguin, 1973).
C. Poster, *The School and the Community* (Macmillan, 1971).
S. Repo, *This Book is About Schools* (Random House, 1970).
A. Sharrock, *Home and School; Select Annotated Bibliography* (NFER, 1971).
J. Stone and F. Taylor, *The Parents' Schoolbook* (Penguin, 1976).
G. Taylor and N. Ayres, *Born and Bred Unequal* (Longman, 1969).
S. Wiseman, *Education and Environment* (Manchester UP, 1964).
M. Young and P. McGeeney, *Learning Begins at Home* (Routledge & Kegan Paul, 1968).